POSITIVELY
BLACK

POSITIVELY
BLACK

Roger D. Abrahams

Prentice-Hall, Inc., Englewood Cliffs, New Jersey

398
A159

13–686097–4
13–686089–3

Library of Congress Catalog Card Number 69–11358

Current Printing (last digit)
10 9 8 7 6 5 4 3 2 1

PRINTED IN THE UNITED STATES OF AMERICA

Prentice-Hall International, Inc., *London*
Prentice-Hall of Australia, Pty. Ltd., *Sydney*
Prentice-Hall of Canada, Ltd., *Toronto*
Prentice-Hall of India Private Limited, *New Delhi*
Prentice-Hall of Japan, Inc., *Tokyo*

Preface

I have been aided in the writing of this book by a number of people, many of whom are acknowledged in the text. The study developed from a paper delivered at a symposium "Folklore and the Social Sciences" sponsored by the Social Science Research Council and the Wenner-Gren Foundation, and I am in debt to both of these organizations and to Jerome Singer who so masterfully organized the symposium. My colleague Américo Parédas was also a participant and a commentator, and his imagination and rigor have helped immeasurably in the expansion of these ideas. As the book went along, Ed Cray was a constant source of energetic assistance, especially in matters of style and argument. He also gave me some of the manuscript texts used as illustrations, as did Richard A. Reuss. I am also indebted to a number of my students in this regard, most notably Weldon Grovey, Patrick Mullen, and Arlette Jones. Mullen also helped greatly in explaining recent developments in Negro music. Our capable secretary Mrs. Francis Lee typed the various versions of the manuscript in her usual good humor. And most remarkable, my wife persisted in good spirits through the depths of this intellectual engagement, remaining a steadfast commentator on matters of ideas and illustrations.

R. D. A.

v

Contents

AN OLD-TIME STORY . . .

Everybody 'round heah is talkin' 'bout 'ligion, gittin' happy an' shoutin'. Theah's one thing 'bout this 'ligion deal I cain't unahstand. I see white people go to church, they got theah at eight o'clock, they out at 'leben. The coloahed man got theah at eight, he's out at two. White man go back at eight o'clock, he's out at nine. Coloahed man got back theah eight o'clock that night, he stays theah til 'leben. An' what I cain't un-ahstand about it is this: the white man goes theah at 'leben an' stays theah till twelve, an' he go fishin', huntin', swimmin', play dominoes, an' shoot a few craps, an wake up the nex' moahnin' an fin' an oil well in his backyahd; the poah coloahed man'll go to wo'k, stay theah all night sayin', "You can have all this worl', but gi'me Jesus," an' wake up the nex' moahnin' an' fin' a "Fo' Rent" sign hangin' on his doah. [1]

AND A NEW ONE

After the Lord had created the Earth, he created the white man, the Mexican, and the Negro. So one day he told them, "Go out and get you some rocks." The white man, being industrious, went out and got a huge rock. The Mexican got a middle-sized rock, and the Negro, being lazy, got a pebble. Later on that evening, the Lord said, "I'm going to turn these rocks into bread." As a result, the white man had a lot of bread, the Mexican had a sufficient amount, but the Negro only had a crumb, and he stayed hungry. So the next day, the Lord again told them the same thing. This time the white man got a great big rock, the Mexican got a little smaller rock, but the Negro brought back a whole half of a mountain. That evening the Lord stood before them and said, "Upon this rock, I will build my church." The Negro said, "You're a mother-fucking liar, you're going to make me some bread." [2]

A Negro Preacher's Prayer:

Lord, we ain't what we oughta be. We ain't what we wanna be. We ain't what we gonna be. But thank God, we ain't what we was.

————*Martin Luther King, Jr.*
To whose memory this book is dedicated

1

Something of a Foreword...

... Afterward

Recently, a Negro teacher from East Texas reported hearing some of her students jumping to the rhyme:

Two, four, six, eight,
We ain't gonna integrate.
Eight, six, four, two,
Bet you sons-of-bitches do. [3] *

Thus the great Civil Rights movement has become enshrined in the oral traditions of the young; the explosiveness of the verbal exchanges between whites and blacks during that time is somehow defused by relegating these sentiments to use in play. But then the sentiments themselves seem so dated in 1968.

It has become clear by this time that integration can no longer be the goal of those who would have Negroes become fully enfranchised citizens of the United States. To be sure, having the right to go to school, or eat, or live wherever one wishes is necessary as a

---

* Bracketed numbers refer to Notes on the Texts, p. 167.

2

preliminary step because it provides Negroes with choices that they didn't have before, and with choice comes a sense of freedom and an ability to find one's own way without being boxed in by social restraint. But integration, we now know, has immediate benefits for such a small percentage of blacks that steps which are more basic and more profound must also be taken.

Just what these steps are, or should be, is now being debated. This book is a document in this debate. It argues that no matter how much energy, time, and money are devoted to bringing Negroes into the mainstream of American life, nothing can be accomplished with sufficient depth and intensity until we have a greater under-standing of black culture. We have been so bent on educating Negroes in *our* ways that we have forgotten that they have their ways too, and we whites need to be educated about them. Because we know so little about Negro culture, we have wasted huge sums of money as well as millions of man hours because in developing pro-grams we have often failed to take into consideration black attitudes toward leadership, energy, time, work, money. We know very little about these matters, even less about black aspirations and ideals. Whites continue to act blindly, ethnocentrically, even those who profess to be on the side of Negroes. Calls go out for two or three hundred thousand new jobs immediately, without specifying what kinds of jobs, or without discerning what ghettoized Negroes think or feel about employment. The government is asked to subsidize hundreds of thousands of new living units when no one has asked blacks what kind of living environment they value most highly. Or if they have been asked, it has been with questions to which blacks have had no meaningful response because the questions were not put in terms understandable to them. We know almost nothing about the information-passing devices of lower-class Negroes. But we do know that they are significantly different from those of middle-class whites (the ones writing the questionnaires).

STEREOTYPING

This is perhaps the greatest problem of blacks in white America—that they are consistently misunderstood because of stereotypic attitudes on the part of whites. This stereotyping, it now seems clear, is as typical of social scientists as racists. And today it is these academic investigators who are being consulted in the formulation of governmental approaches. Thus, the student of black America must live with the knowledge that whatever information and conclusions he comes up with may be used by nonprofessionals, individuals interested in furthering a plan of social action (or inaction, depending upon how you look at it). Yet on looking at the history of the black problem and the ways in which scholars' data and conclusions have been presented and used, it becomes obvious that the academic generally has been just as unconscious of his motives and just as caught up in the tides of public sentiment as the politician or the man-on-the-street. He has thereby often exhibited the same patterns of thought, rested his arguments on the same unexamined assumptions, and been unconsciously drawn to the same stereotype traits as those with less knowledge about blacks. (And I do not exclude myself from the burden of these remarks.)

Unfortunately, such a schooled investigator is not just another human being, he is one who is regarded as an expert in the field and who is consulted in discussions on the subject. He therefore cannot afford to resign responsibility for his arguments and even his data. The mask of objectivity must be understood for what it is—in the main, just a mask, a pose assumed by the writer-observer to make informed argument more persuasive.

In most cases, the social scientist's failure to recognize that he is unconsciously falling into these habits of mind makes little difference, for who listens to him but other members of his discipline? But in matters concerning blacks in America, his work, though usually in diluted form, is used to affect public attitudes and sometimes even governmental policy. That this does happen and has occurred recently is admirably set forth in the remarkable document by Lee Rainwater and William L. Yancey called *The Moynihan Report and the Politics of Controversy*. Here is set forth exactly how, in one crucial case, the accumulated ideas and data of a generation of scholars were brought to bear, at one point in time, on the formulation of governmental policy. And here is presented one of the greatest object lessons on why social scientists should bear in mind that their researches may be so used, that they may therefore go to as great lengths as possible to examine their own motives and patterns of thought and to present their conclusions with clear discussion of assumptions and social implications.

The great virtue of the Rainwater and Yancey book is that it enables us to see the Moynihan Report for exactly what it was—a governmental polemic intended to be read by only a few officials who would act on it in the formulation of governmental policy. Its subsequent publication was an afterthought, but it has proved to be more important than its intended more limited uses. In retrospect, its publication seems to mark a crucial point in the reformulation of black attitudes and black tactics. Intended to bring together the force of public opinion and scholarly argument, and therefore to provide a focus by which Civil Rights efforts would be regularized and built into all governmental programs aimed at blacks, the Moynihan Report seems to have had the opposite effect, at least in the attitudes and actions of Afro-Americans. To blacks reacting to the document, it showed Moynihan to be the whitest of whites. Ironically it caused a widespread realization that there was a new *bête noire* in the black cause, the culture-blind white liberal.

Moynihan committed a fault of argument so egregiously ethnocentric that he provided his critics with an efficient model of argument against the entire liberal establishment. Specifically, Moynihan chose to focus on the supposed disintegration of the Negro family in order to provide the government with a standard against which to test the effectiveness of all programs aimed at the betterment of blacks. He wished to have the government test all programs in terms of what they would do to change the basic disabilities of the Negro family system, that is, to make the black family unit more nearly approximate that of middle-class whites, specifically by providing more jobs for black men.

Moynihan says this as boldly as possible in his opening statement:

> At the heart of the deterioration of the fabric of Negro society is the deterioration of the Negro family.
> It is this fundamental source of the weakness of the Negro community at the present time. . . .

> The white family has achieved a high degree of stability and is maintaining that stability.
>
> By contrast, the family structure of lower class Negroes is highly unstable, and in many urban centers is approaching complete breakdown.

It is obvious to anyone who works with Negroes that they have a family system and that it has been remarkably stable, at least in terms of its configuration. It is unstable only when judged by the white ideals of the husband-wife-child relationship–complex. Even more important is Moynihan's assumption that the stable family is the only social unit in which a child can effectively learn, thereby completely disregarding the tremendous amount of positive learning about society which takes place on the streets, in interaction with peers.

But in judging the Moynihan argument, Rainwater and Yancey rightly insist that we bear in mind who Moynihan's audience was and how he was trying to affect them, as well as what the historical and social situation was that led him to formulate his ideas. He was confronted, because of the passage of the 1964 Civil Rights Bill, with a sudden sapping of the energies of the Civil Rights movement, and he felt strongly that the most important work was yet to come. He therefore needed a crisis document to refocus government attentions, and so he formulated his report in crisis terms. But these very terms allow us to see, highlighted, the weaknesses of the liberal approach that Moynihan represents so fully.

The Moynihan Report rang down the curtain on the Civil Rights movement, though that was hardly its intent. It brought to a head the arguments of leading social scientists and those of political liberals. The two had differed only in the texture of their arguments, not in their content or intentions. Both had sought to augment the efforts of the Civil Rights decade that highlighted the terrible conditions of black existence and by this to bring about legal action by which existing but covert government sanctions for these conditions were eliminated. To do this, through the efforts of scholarship, certain aspects of black culture and the black condition had to be dramatized: the Negro lack of emotional and institutional stability, their essential disorganization, their proclivity for delinquency and a life of crime, their bad educational and work records, their disrespect for health services and birth control, and so on. The object of stressing these features was to expose the social causes for the Negro condition, but the result, as seen in retrospect, was to republish the Negro stereotype in only slightly more positive terms than those used by the detractors of blacks.

Nowhere do we see this well-meaning rationale for the stereotype so clearly as in Stanley M. Elkins' much read study, *Slavery*. Elkins, in his rush to rationalize the existence of the "Sambo" stereotype, compares the psychological conditions of slavery with those of prisoners in concentration camps. Noting that these prisoners strongly identify with their captors and consequently go through an involved series of self-debasement procedures, Elkins provides a psychological justification for the personality of those Negroes who conform to the stereotype. The faults of his theory are especially dangerous because his essays have been so widely read and followed. Most important is that Elkins totally accepts as fact that Negroes subscribed to the stereotype, without bothering to investigate how this role was played and how blacks learned to use the stereotype as an aggressive device by which they could fight back. It seems clear that in most cases, blacks have found it convenient to wear the mask of Sambo; they have developed upon numerous traditional techniques by which they may successfully aggress in both covert and overt fashion. The Sambo, then, often was not a personality-type as much as a convenient mask to wear; in assuming this role consciously or reflexively, blacks could achieve aggression and protection at the same time.

Elkins, one of those relied upon by Moynihan, is representative of the social scientists of the Civil Rights era. The task of that age was to dramatize the conditions of slavery that had persisted into the 20th century and to underline their demoralizing and dysfunctional effects. The scholars of that decade were successful in providing ample evidence for the widely-disseminated reports by which the public was made increasingly aware of the black condition; they helped create the atmosphere that brought about important legislative and judicial changes.

However, with passage of the Civil Rights Act of 1964, a change occurred in the struggle, one which led to a feeling of complacency on the part of both Congress and many workers in the cause of Civil Rights. It was evident to Moynihan, and to most others working with economically disadvantaged Negroes, that the battle was anything but over. The black bourgeoisie had profited tremendously from this victory, but the plight of the ghettoized masses was, if anything, worsened. Furthermore, one of the unplanned offshoots of the struggle was that the stereotype image of blacks, far from being exorcised, had been re-emphasized, though in a new, sentimentalized positive stereotype form.

This was only vaguely sensed at the time, however. The struggle for the enunciation of an Afro-American identity had only begun, but the problem seemed to be that there was nothing in the air that would permit the proper refocussing of the trouble. Then came the Moynihan Report which highlighted, in most extreme form, the essentially stereotypic method of argument that had been used in the past. The approach was so dramatically ethnocentric and betrayed such an ignorance of the actual texture of black life that the Report provided just the target which the movement needed. Though the Report was framed with the best intentions, blacks saw the document as providing a rallying cry and came to regard it as the epitome of what was wrong in the thinking of their white, liberal fellow-travelers. Moynihan had made it onto the black shit-list in spite of his obvious sympathies, and Afro-American militancy found itself launched into a new era in which the black became beautiful and the white became nothing but a honky and a paddy.

It is, of course, difficult to determine whether the existence of the Report signalled the beginning of the new age, or whether its appearance simply provided a convenient pushing-off point. The paradox remains that the Moynihan Report did the very thing it set out to do—influence governmental attitude—but it did so at the very time when this way of thinking and formulating programs was no longer representative of the attitudes of the most vocal blacks about themselves and their future. Its publication therefore caused a division of opinion that Moynihan could not have predicted; Moynihan was saying things that at least President Johnson was prepared to listen to and to embody in speeches and programs, but in the eyes of black militants this became a further instance of stereotypic thinking and therefore a point of view that had to be rejected.

ABOUT-FACE

With the issuing of the Report came its rejection and the formulation of a new black position which seeks to reject the negative aspects of the stereotype in favor of the many more positive features of black life. The problem then becomes one of changing attitude toward blacks and constructing a new image of them. This about-face is very hard for scholars to perform, because to do so is to admit that they too have been operating in terms of the Negro stereotype, and therefore playing into the hands of racists, if not becoming racists themselves. However, there have been recent trends in the reporting of black life indicating that the about-face has at least begun.

The result of the change of image is just now being felt in social science as it has for four years in black militant politics. Reacting against this image of the perpetually downtrodden, blacks are increasingly discussing the ways by which they have managed to persist, how they have adapted to changing circumstances, circumstances inevitably coercive and dominating, developing techniques by which they not only endure but flourish. And in all this they have been actively searching for the African elements of their lives that have persisted and have been adapted to their changing place in society. This changed image is beginning to invade the social science literature, causing a refocussing there away from the conception of a culture of poverty and deprivation to one of a group that is diverse and strong and has integrity. For instance, this perspective is boldly and clearly stated in a recent book, *Black Families in White America*, written by a black sociologist, Andrew Billingsley.

> The Negro family must have a central place in this process of social evolution. In this respect, our own view is consistent with that expressed by Daniel P. Moynihan in his several writings and public appearances. But unlike Moynihan and others, we do not view the Negro family as a causal nexus in a "tangle of pathology" which feeds on itself. Rather we view the Negro family in

theoretical perspective as a sub-system of the larger society. It is . . . an absorbing, adaptive, and amazingly resilient mechanism for the socialization of its children and the civilization of its society (p. 33).

So just as the Civil Rights movement found its academic champions, the Era of Black Militancy has already found its apologists. A group of investigators of black culture is arising, answering the need of the Negro masses for data that will show black life to be suffused not with dysfunction but with meaningful organizations and communications systems, not with an institutional life in decay but with a set of ordering social devices that are tenacious and successful, and that will show that blacks themselves are not a group of depressed and shattered people but a vibrant and creative set of individuals.

This book has been written in an effort to educate whites about certain aspects of Negro culture that seem essential to an understanding of lower-class black life. In doing this we look at the things Negroes say, and have said in the past, about the texture and qualities of their lives.

Like so many other studies now being spewed out onto the beleaguered reading public, this study arose out of the crisis conditions created by the riots. It began with some students asking me for an explanation of the riots based on my knowledge of urban Negroes, as I had lived in a ghetto for two years. I had to explain that, as a folklorist, I could not explain why the riots happened, but that I might be able to explain why Negroes decided to express themselves dramatically through the agency of the riots. In other words, I could not explain why these holocausts occur when and where they do, but I might be able to cast some light on the cultural experience and expressions of blacks in America, and I can point out some relationships between these cultural expressions and the riots. But soon the riots became less and less important, and other active aspects of black life came to be emphasized. The riots do have certain features in common with other kinds of lower-class Negro performances, but no extensive treatment of these similarities will be made. I will be concerned with the dynamics of performances and of pieces performed by lower-class Negroes. I will, but only by implication, also be concerned with the psychological dynamics of a people who may take to rioting. It is tempting to relate the two dynamics as they seem to reflect so much the same attitudes and styles, but to do this is far beyond my competence.

The United States, in spite of its democratic ideals, is essentially a pluralistic state; that is, rather than being a true "melting pot" ours is a nation in which communities with widely differing cultural perspectives only coexist. They are able to persist as separate cultural enclaves because one culture is dominant and the others, perforce, subordinate. This means not only that we have second-class citizenship from the political and social point of view, but that the basis of this discrimination is cultural. This is more insidious because it is often unconscious and results in inequities that go unrecognized.

COMMUNICATION

These cultural inequities are proclaimed and maintained by the creation of stereotypes. Stereotypes arise in almost any culture-contact situation. They are a response of an anxiety experienced by both groups involved, and they are developed on both sides. Stereotypes focus on those very areas in which the two groups most often make contact. But rather than directing themselves at the communication inherent in the contact situation, the stereotype emphasizes those places where communication is impossible because the group doing things doesn't do things correctly or it doesn't have the right attitude toward matters of extreme importance to the group imposing the stereotype. A stereotype will always exhibit the bias of the group that fashions it.

A classic case of communications failure arising out of the mutual imposition of stereotypes by two cultures coming into contact is discussed by Erving Goffman in his analysis of what he calls "interaction ritual":

> The Western traveler used to complain that the Chinese could never be trusted to say what they meant but always said what they felt their Western listener wanted to hear. The Chinese used to complain that the Westerner was brusque, boorish, and un-

mannered. In terms of Chinese standards, presumably, the conduct of a Westerner is so gauche that he creates an emergency [of maintaining face], forcing the Asian to forgo any kind of direct reply in order to rush in with a remark that might rescue the Westerner from the compromising position in which he has placed himself (p. 17n).

Here the Chinese and the Westerner have confronted each other with different modes of personal interaction, and because the two cultures carried different senses of decorum there resulted an impairment of communication and the beginning of stereotype configurations on both sides. Stereotypes so often begin in this way, focussing upon different communications-decorum systems. The New World Negro has often been called garrulous and unrestrained in his linguistic behavior by whites with whom he has come into constant contact because, in certain situations, he continued to use the elaborate mode of address system brought by him from Africa. Typical in this regard are the comments made by the English traveler, John Stewart, in the 19th century, in his book *A View of the Past and Present State of Jamaica*:

> Although the proverbial sayings of negroes have often much point and meaning, they, however, no sooner begin to expatiate and enter more minutely into particulars, than they become tedious, verbose, and circumlocutory, beginning their speeches with a tiresome exordium, mingling with them much extraneous matter, and frequently traversing over and over the same ground, and cautioning the hearer to be attentive, as if fearful that some of the particulars and points on which their meaning and argument hinged should escape his attention. So that by the time they arrive at the peroration of their harangue, the listener is heartily fatigued with it, and perceives the whole which has been said, though it may have taken up half an hour, could have been comprised in half-a-dozen words (p. 264).

Clearly we have here an instance of failure of communication on the deepest level, for the Negro was using what he thought to be the mode of address most appropriate to the occasion, but he was condemned rather than appreciated for this act of decorum.

Another more recent instance of this type of intercultural failure of communication between whites and Negroes is the "problem" encountered by white teachers of Negro children of eye-avertance. In many Negro communities young children have learned that meeting an older person's gaze is a sign of hostility or defiance. Therefore, when called upon by the teacher in class, they look away from her when responding. If the question asked is not directed to the individual student, the teacher will tend not to notice the direction of the gaze. But if the question is directed at a specific student, the eye-avertance will commonly be interpreted by the teacher as evidence that something sneaky has been going on, or that the student is being arrogant or disrespectful. This is an especially great problem for speech therapists, for they must often have the child watch their lip movements. One inventive therapist recognized the source of the problem and has learned to have the child look into a mirror at her reflection, thus preserving decorum while serving efficiency.

Cultural differences of this sort, when encountered in the contact situation, contribute heavily to the development of a stereotype. Stereotype is a configuration of traits that are imputed to a group, that serve to categorize members of that group in terms of peculiarities, differences, "characteristics." But as the above examples show, these characteristics are often imputed more out of misunderstanding of practices than through the practices themselves or the attitudes that lie behind them. This misunderstanding is unfortunate in any circumstance because of the failures of communication engendered by the stereotype; but it is even more distressing when, as in the United States, it is encountered between groups in a culturally pluralistic situation, for then it is used by the dominant group as a means of maintaining status.

This subordination is engineered by imputing cultural practices to the minority which are deviant, blasphemous, or immoral. To state the procedure a little more positively, stereotyping is a means of illustrating the ideals of one group by pointing to places where other groups seem to negate them. A stereotype, as we most commonly understand the term, is the result of a negative typing procedure in which those attitudes and activities which are valued and which are threatened because of unconscious forces within the group are put into negative form and projected onto the other group (Williams, p. 40). In most cases, this must simply be regarded as the way in which disparate groups react to each other, and therefore it is a phenomenon which, in our shrinking world, is something to regret. But in cases where the two groups live side by side, as with blacks and whites, and they are served by the same government and economic systems, the procedure becomes dangerous as a barrier to communications.

Furthermore, the stereotyped group is stigmatized. By imputing negative traits to Negroes and then by telling stories in illustration, whites have learned to enjoy vicariously the Negro's supposed freedom from social constraint, and to reject the blacks for these same characteristics. Unless we are willing to learn to understand other cultures in our midst, thus breaking down this kind of stereotyped thinking, we will be incapable of fulfilling our professed high intentions.

This study is an attempt to break down the stereotype of the American Negro by exploring certain aspects of Negro culture that commonly, when encountered by whites, bring about a stereotype response. To do this it is necessary to look at what that stereotype is and how it undermines efforts at integration, however well-intentioned those efforts might be. Many of the effects are self-evident, or have been commented upon so often that to repeat the arguments would be impractical and self-defeating. Rather, I would like to focus on ways in which the ethnocentric attribution of stereotype traits have operated in perhaps the most important realm of the American experience—in education.

BIAS IN SCHOOLS

Our educational system could hardly be more efficiently designed to perpetuate the status of Negroes than it is today. No institution in our country is more middle-class in its biases nor more blind to its ethnocentricities. There are certain traits of the Negro stereotype with which educators of the young have little commerce. For instance, the imputed supersexuality of blacks can hardly be attributed to the Negro child—though most teachers of lower-class Negro children have stories about the filthy sexual language of some black child. Furthermore, childishness and animality, with their accompanying immorality, can hardly be imputed to Negro children alone —though most of these teachers will, if prodded, give you stories about how *certain* black children have come to school without any notion of table manners or even toilet training, but they'll hasten to tell you that they have white children who have the same problems. But certain stereotype attitudes recur and have a great effect on the educability of the child: specifically, his inability to use the language, his lack of cultural background on which to build "basic understanding," and his unwillingness to communicate. ("They just sit there surly and won't say a thing—they won't even look at you.")

LANGUAGE

One of the statements most often repeated by white elementary teachers about "them"—their Negro charges—is that they have no verbal resources and, because of this, no language ability. This is commonly followed by one of two rationalizing statements: either "these poor children have never been taught to speak correctly" or "they couldn't have developed verbal skills since they come from families with so many children that there isn't any time for communication with their parents." ("Why some of them don't even know who their fathers are!") Both of these statements are ethnocentric in the extreme, even if they are well-meaning.

In regard to the supposed substandard language of lower-class Negroes, schooled investigators are just beginning to recognize that Negro speech is not a dialect of English at all but rather part of a language system unto itself which differs from "standard" English in everything but vocabulary. Probably originating from an African Portuguese Creole language, New World Negro dialects developed through a substitution of the vocabularies of the speech of the dominant culture in the places the slaves were deposited (Whinnom). In the United States, rather than viewing the various types of Negro speech as different dialectal corruptions of English, it is more meaningful to view them as one creole language, whole unto itself, which has been progressively gravitating toward the regional

English dialects with which it has come into contact (William Stewart). This English creole is not a language *manqué* but a communications system which is as fully developed as any other language. Only by an unfortunate historical accident has it accrued the vocabulary of English, and therefore appeared to many observers as an English dialect. What this means for teachers is that they must learn to deal with the teaching of Standard English as if it were a different language, but one in which most (but not all, by any means) of the vocabulary is the same.

Furthermore—and this is what I will be documenting in this book—there is not only a different language at work here but a different attitude toward speech and speech acts. We are just beginning to recognize that we don't know very much about information-passing among Negroes; but we can predict with a reasonable degree of accuracy that the subjects and methods of communication of knowledge and feeling will be quite different from white middle-class norms. The implications of such differences are of obvious importance to teachers of Negroes, especially since they have been operating on the assumption that no cultural differences existed in this area.

One of the basic variations in the passing on of information is in regard to who communicates with whom, and in what recurrent situations; this brings us back to the second ethnocentric judgment commonly made by teachers—that Negro children are not verbal because they don't have a chance to communicate with parents. This attitude makes the assumption that the only communication channel useful for educational development is that which arises between adults and children. This is a natural outgrowth of the image that teachers have of themselves (ratified by the community, of course) that they are surrogate parents. But with children who are not subject to the middle-class family system, this places them immediately at a disadvantage, both in relation to the teacher who has these expectations, and in regard to the educational system in general.

The fact is that most of the lower-class black children who come into the classroom have a well-developed sense of language and its power to pass on information and to control interpersonal relationships; but the children derive this language skill not from social interaction with adults (with whom they have been taught to be silent) so much as with other children. This situation is dictated by the custom of care, in which younger children are placed in the care of older ones; it is also assisted by the practice of street play which has older children teaching the younger both verbal and motor play routines. In this milieu, children learn the power of words in the development of their sense of self. They learn the importance of banter, the power of the taunt, the pleasure of playing with words. They develop vocabulary and other skills in active contest situations, for the purpose of winning a verbal game and gaining esteem from their group. If they have little informational exchange with adults, they have a great deal of language-learning play with fellow children, a factor usually ignored in the classroom. Indeed, Negro children find, when they go into school, that the language skills they have learned are in a tongue that is despised as substandard and performed in a manner that is regarded as hostile, obscene, or arrogant. They learn very quickly that the easiest way of getting by in the classroom is to be quiet—and so they are accused of being nonverbal. This derogation of language and language skills, furthermore, does little for the development of self-confidence.

If this weren't enough, even the best-intentioned language arts teachers commonly carry a further prejudice into the educational encounter with black pupils. It is firmly felt by them that reading is a skill that is the key to learning, that words are *things* that one must learn to recognize on the printed page or blackboard because such recognition will open up the repositories of knowledge, books. The often unconscious assumption made by these teachers is that all children will share the attitude that books are valuable things. But not only do most lower-class Negro children not share this feeling (since like most lower-class people most never encounter much reading material around the house or on the streets) but they don't commonly recognize words as things. Words to them are rather devices to be used in performances. Consequently, the argument that one must learn to read and then write in order to find one's way into the wonderful world of books is totally lost on children from such a background. They have not been concerned with the kinds of information contained in books, the kind that middle-class adults pass on to children, and that teachers expect to feed students.

But this does not mean that the lower-class black child brings no cultural resources into the classroom—they are just *different* resources. He brings a verbal skill, which, if recognized by the teacher, can be of considerable value in the development of an understanding of language. But to capitalize upon this fund, the child must be allowed to speak, even if this violates the usual sense of decorum the teacher carries into class with her. The teacher must further learn to understand the communication system with which she is dealing, both as it relates to adult-child situations and to those between peers. Once this system is recognized it appears obvious (as it did to Herbert Kohl when he taught Harlem children) that one can teach writing by showing the children how much more permanent and pleasurable are their verbal performances when written down. Once the value of words as records of speech events has been shown, the reading of other people's performances in book form will come naturally. By attacking the problem this way, the teacher will have served education in two ways. First, the child has been allowed to develop his own resources without having them exhibited as substandard; therefore he has been permitted to retain and develop his self-respect. Second, he has been to taught to speak in an appropriate classroom manner (giving him a sense of the appropriateness of different kinds of language), then write, and then read, and he has thus been lead to a point where he has been offered a cultural choice. He has learned to recognize alternatives and to make discretions, which I understand are the aims of our educational process. All of this has been achieved through a recognition of cultural variability on the part of the teacher. The only way this can be achieved, however, is through an understanding of the cultural heritage of the black children (and by this heritage, I *don't* mean spirituals or jazz, but those expressions of culture that the children know from their own immediate experience). The only way this cultural relativity can be learned is by breaking through the barriers to understanding erected by stereotyped thinking.

This book is concerned with the subject of stereotypes beyond trying to dispel certain white notions of Negroes. It also focuses upon Negroes' ways of typing themselves, both as a group in open contest with whites and as different personality types in contest with each other. Since I am a folklorist, this book is primarily made up of analyses of expressive—rather than the usual institutional—culture; but this approach seems essential to an understanding of American Negro life-ways because of the central importance of performers and performances in the everyday life of blacks.

Most of the expressive materials here are fictions, in story or song. These imaginative productions utilize the same kind of typing procedure as stereotyping; however, in expressive materials, typing serves as an agency of artistic economy. All fictions deal in character-types which we can recognize immediately without too great a description. Folklore, especially, deals with "stock-characters" given the very public nature of its oral performance. But there is an easily demonstrable relationship between stock-characters and stereotype-figures, for the two are often identical. And, as noted above, fictions that draw upon stereotypes can be the most virulent means for proclaiming the stereotype, for they enlist the devices of wit and significant order to call attention to themselves as performances; while doing so, they also call attention to stereotype notions.

However, though all such fictions involve the use of stock characters, not all deal in stereotype figures. In most cases, the characters and their actions are not used to publish prejudice but merely to point to social types that exist within the group. In such cases, material that deals with such social types can be used to investigate the group's own sense of social structure, and their own concepts of what constitutes deviance and immorality. This book will not only make an assault on certain white prejudices, but it will also show how blacks themselves have handled the white stereotype, and how Negroes see themselves as a conglomeration of social types.

I can not emphasize too highly that this is not just a book full of Negro folklore. The impulse to study and dramatize speech events such as these goes beyond a folklore professor's simple fascination with words and patterns of performance. We are confronted, in the

United States, with a situation of constant misunderstandings between whites and blacks, constant misreadings of intentions and effects. These failures of communication all too often lead to the widening of a social gap which threatens the foundations of our existence as a nation. But these are great times precisely because the foundations *are* being threatened, because our basic cultural assumptions are being questioned and tested. The unrest on our campuses is certainly a result of this questioning procedure, and of the failure of our conventional answers to provide any sense of satisfaction. It is clear in my mind that the sense of anxiety which is rampant arises from student confrontation with a square world and the straight life—that is, with an environment which promises a rather limited range of approved activities and attitudes. This comes, significantly, at the very moment when we are, because of our humanistic education, in a good position to understand the tremendous variety of life styles, of roles and masks that are available to us if we choose to take them on. The square world rejects this diversity; it insists on viewing life in an outmoded and essentially ethnocentric perspective.

But fortunately for our collective cultural sanity we have a home-grown and constant reminder of diversity and possible choice. Living in our midst, and in numbers far too great to ignore, are blacks who remind us with every word, movement, gesture, that we are a culturally heterogeneous country. Further, we are so attuned to tapping creative sources of black culture without paying our dues to the club that the threat that this creativity will be eliminated from our lives is unsettling in the extreme. In our stereotype we have made blacks into paradoxical creatures, incurable creative entertainers, and irretrievably chaotic, violent, and destructive types. Essentially, these traits point to the tremendous fund of energy in the black world, energy that fascinates and troubles us. Normally fascination is the dominant sentiment, and we do not hesitate to share in and borrow from this creative exuberance. But when this energy takes what we deem to be a violent expression it scares us— not just because we are threatened by the violence, but because the pipeline to this fund of creativity is in danger of being severed.

Inherent in any black artistic expression is the threat of exclusiveness and exclusion, and this the square world can ill afford. This is why black talk, especially the playful badinage of *jiving*, threatens the straight world, and why *gaming* behavior which seems so insincere is rejected by its denizens. But rather than scaring whites into learning to understand the most extremely black forms of black expression, this kind of word-play causes the opposite reaction— intense rejection and the retreat into the dim recesses of the pure white bag. We see this clearly in the rejection of the most publicly coercive black men-of-words, Malcolm X, Adam Clayton Powell, Stokely Carmichael, Eldridge Cleaver, and our American martyr-saint, Muhammed Ali.

Clearly the threat of another way of talking, another way of performing has driven us to a point of cultural crisis that we are not willing to face up to. Too long we have relied on the taste of this fountain while maintaining that its source is of no importance. Too long have we culturally bought and stolen without being made to feel the consequences. But now blacks are dunning us for our over-drafts by more publicly entertaining us but in terms we don't understand. The voice is too loud, no longer crooning; the actions are no longer so smooth and so rhythmic, no longer danced out.

If these sounds and these movements threaten us, they also present an alternative that could provide us with an ever-increasing store of alternative style, creative acts. But to accept this we must learn to understand a new language and new cultural options. We must accept the burdens and potentials of choice that arise out of our experiences of cultural diversity. The choice is an awful one, but only because its promises are so great and the present retreat from the choice so pronounced on the part of a large segment of America, both white and black.

By taking our option, though, we can do so much for ourselves and also, I am convinced, for blacks. Many blacks themselves show an often-defeating ambivalence about black expressive culture; they have been told for so many years that they have no culture or that what they do have is childish or degenerate; this approach is still accepted by many blacks. At this point in black history, the need for pride and cultural identity is obvious; this blacks can and will give themselves, but whites can help by learning to understand

and value the basic precepts—not just the external manifestations—of black performances. So the black problem really *is* a white problem, a white failure of understanding in a situation in which we must have available channels of communication. We have been calling for a massive educational effort for blacks, but understanding can not arise until there is an equally massive campaign of education about black culture for whites.

This work then is aimed at whites. But it is important to point out that it takes a point of view that is shared by some black intellectuals and is actively contested by others. On the one hand, it runs contrary to the very forceful arguments put forth by Ralph Ellison that so-called Negro culture is just one version of American culture because the United States since its beginnings has been strongly affected by Afro-American cultural manifestations (especially expressive devices) and has internalized them in a meaningful way. Mr. Ellison is certainly correct in this, but by emphasizing these features of acculturation he neglects those broad and important areas in which blacks are seen as different and those in which they see themselves as diverse from middle-class America. To underline the shared cultural patterns at the expense of this creative and destructive disparity is to ignore that delicious sense of cultural alternatives available in America.

On the other hand, there are those blacks who would reject the street-corner culture that I discuss herein because it is part of the life lived in the depths to which whites have forced Negroes to sink. These militants argue that we have a black culture only because blacks have not been permitted access to those features of American affluence and power that go along with white middle-class culture. Perhaps the devices discussed throughout this book are only defensive ones and will pass with the need for defensiveness, something to be achieved through changing the power structure of American society. Though there is a good deal of truth to this argument, the pursuit of it provides a disservice to Negroes, because it intensifies guilts and insecurities for the black masses who are born into, and who continue to express elements of this culture. It serves the revolution, it seems to me, but not the masses.

But even more important, at least from my point of view, these aggressive-defensive devices developed under the conditions of sub-ordination make lower-class blacks the ethnic group in America best equipped to handle certain contemporary cultural threats. These problems arise from the assault of change, brought about by the effects of technological developments, upon certain elements of culture. In a world in which experiences of cultural diversity are becoming more available and inevitable, there is a constant threat of the dissolution of one's own culture. Some can face alternative cultural styles, others can not. And rejection of alternatives too often results in blind ethnocentric attitudes. If cultural assault is the keynote of the future, blacks already have time-tested devices to handle such problems. To ask them to reject these is to denude both them and American life in general of important mechanisms of cultural defense and adaptation. Furthermore, I don't think that any amount of preaching is going to get most black Americans to give these things up. Rather, they seem to be seizing upon them and developing them more highly if sometimes more self-consciously.

But there is a further reason why I think this militant point of view needs challenging. This position has provided one of the major assumptions of sociologists dealing with the ghetto situation: that when lower-class blacks become middle-class, presumably through a growth in income and advancement potential, these cultural dif-ferences disappear. In other words, this argument supposes that not only are these cultural mechanisms a result of a coercive social situation, but they persist only as long as the economic structure continues. But my experience and observations would contradict this assumption, at least in part.

First of all, this assumption has been made before we have under-stood that we have here a culturally pluralistic situation. We have therefore assumed that the upward mobile black eschews a life style as he makes more money and can move from the ghetto situation. We have done this without really investigating the characteristics of this life style, especially in its expressive dimension. There is a great deal of truth to the observation that a cultural leap is made, as well as a social one, when the ghetto is left behind. But there are, in my experience, many aspects of black culture that are taken along, especially in the area of social perspective. I notice this because the joke repertoire of the streetman and the members of the black bourgeoisie share a great deal. The same kind of stories persist, illustrating the same rhetorical point of view. Even more important is the persistence of the respect for "good talk" in an informal social situation (i.e. out of the institutional milieu of school or church). I am not arguing that there are no cultural changes in such a situation—obviously there are many—but that some of the cultural differences described in this essay persist, sometimes in active use, sometimes as an unstated but deeply felt cultural resource. This becomes important, for many black militants, who in most regards would have to be considered middle-class in their intellectual perspective, are finding themselves, in "soul sounds," in the songs and stories of lower-class "brothers," in the values and the coping devices that they can both appreciate and use. This is, to be sure, more true of black men than women in the militant movement, but many of the texts used here are from women, indicating that sexual differences are also not as extreme as we have supposed.

The object of this work, then, is to underline the cultural difference between lower-class blacks and the rest of America, a difference that must be understood if we are truly to accept these blacks into the mainstream of American life. But we also must understand this culture because it has provided us with so much of the creative vitality by which *we* have kept going.

All of this is an introduction, and one that seems to rival in length the work itself. So as one of my black friends in Philadelphia always remarked on leaving: " 'Nough said, Ted."

2

For Garban Tivoli Godrick and a few of his buddies, it had been one continuous party. In the garage where he lived a variety of stolen merchandise was scattered about—transistor radios, a movie camera, a .22 rifle, shoes, and clothing, and bottle after bottle of liquor. As dawn broke Monday morning, a quartet of youths were lolling around, exhausted, slightly high, but, for the first time in their lives, feeling as if they had accomplished something. They could not say why they felt that way; they could not say what it was that filled the void that before had made a shell of their bodies. They only knew that, never having known success of any kind before, this they could call success. . . .

"Man, that was the meanest little cop I ever did see" [one] said. " 'Nigger boy,' he said to me, 'how'd you like to meet your maker right now?' He had these little pin-pricky eyes and I said to myself, shit man! This character ain't fooling! So I said, 'No sir, I sure wouldn't. I was just on my way home from Bible class when I seen all these people,' and I makes it up to him like I don't really cotton to all this stuff. So he says, 'Well, nigger boy, you go on back and you tell all those black motherfuckers down there we gonna come and blow 'em up!' And then he stops the car, and gives me a kick that I thinks puts me all the way across the freeway!"

"Shit, man! You got no soul. I'd 'a told that white motherfucker to fly up his own ass! The days of Old Black Joe and Aunt Jemima done gone!"

"Yeah. Well you and Old Black Joe'd be playing Georgia Skin

26

together in heaven, and I'm here!" *
They all laugh.
"The police, they real mad now. I seen 'em come down on the set last night, shootin' shotguns and bustin' stuff and all! They real mad!"
"Yeah, man. Like they knows we beat 'em good. They put them nationals in here, but that don't mean nothing! They know anytime we wants, we can beat 'em" (Conot).**

Robert Conot's *Rivers of Blood, Years of Darkness* is one of a few reports of conversations of rioters about the riots. His description above dramatizes some of the performance values and ambivalences which are evident not just during riots but in every interpersonal encounter with most black ghetto dwellers.

One of the aspects of lower-class Negro life as an oral culture, which is least understood by middle-class society is the way in which everyday life is suffused with play. In an environment such as the ghettos, *gaming* or the art of the *put-on* suffuses interpersonal relations. Thus all public activities have a tendency to gravitate toward performances, and this is as true of the riots as any other action.

The rest of Conot's riot scene proceeds with gaming accounts of conflicts with the police and National Guard in which the "bloods"— the "soul people"—come off best each time. The earnest regard for effective performance by those involved is self-evident. But this dimension of the riots, and of black ghetto-life in general, has almost never been recognized by whites, except in the snide terms of those policemen who described the riots as "just one big nigger Saturday night."

AMERICA: TWO VIEWS

The shock of the riots to most Americans was that they happened at all, and that they could continue to happen, a shock not unlike that arising from civil war in any Western nation. In our culture

* For these opposed approaches to life-problems, see the "cat-gorilla" controversy in Chapter 4.
** Reprinted with the publisher's permission from *Rivers of Blood, Years of Darkness* (copyright © 1967 by Bantam Books, Inc., all rights reserved).

such conflict is, by definition, convulsive and disruptive, serious and unreasonable; internal warfare is totally out of line with our vision of ourselves as members of a balanced and ordered society which has a built-in sense of social equilibrium. We feel that our system has an answer to any expression of imbalance through legislation, adjudication, or election.

Our conception of ourselves as social creatures gravitates toward a utopian view of society, as the sociologist Ralf Dahrendorf has suggested; and utopias are societies in which change is absent. Alterations may occur, but they have been envisaged in the overall design. Any process of life, social or otherwise, is viewed in a utopia in terms of recurrent patterns—a vision of life known as "pastoral" to literary critics, especially when it relies on attuning existence to the cycle of nature. Even anti-utopias (embodiments of systems we fear) are conceived in the same self-contained terms, as being consistent and all of a piece. "We," says Dahrendorf of sociologists, "have constructed the 'social system.' In the end . . . we are left with a perfect society which has structure, is functioning, is in equilibrium, and is therefore just" (Dahrendorf, 1958, p. 119).

But it is not just sociologists who are prone to conceptualizing society in such balanced terms; this vision seems to predominate in the most dearly held systems of belief in the United States: democracy, egalitarianism, even capitalism as it is conceived on the popular level, through such slogans as "the law of supply and demand." At the very heart of "The American Dream" is the idea of a place and an "equal opportunity" for everyone; and all of our national political and social apothegms, like "of the people, by the people, for the people," and "regardless of creed, color, or national origin," and even "a chicken in every pot" announce a balanced social ideal with a progressive bias that says that if equality doesn't exist now its possibility is built into the system. Though we are constantly forced to recognize that disharmony exists in our society, we seem convinced that we have techniques in the machinery of our system of government and economics to bring about harmony, and we work toward this by attempting to expand our social "space" so that it may include within its ordered boundaries those who are now outside wanting in. This is why we abhor "extremists" and vote for "moderates," while concerning ourselves about where the "American political mainstream" is located.

Anathema to our popular sense of social order is the idea of coercion. The anti-utopias that we envisage and the enemies that we recognize are conceived in terms of powers potentially coercive, in terms of communist and fascist societies that would force those living under these systems to adjust to an order that they themselves have neither proposed nor imagined.

Rejecting the idea of government by coercion, we conceive of society popularly in terms of some natural, but ideal, order toward which we are constantly progressing. This platonic equilibrium model is, and has been, very useful in providing us with a sense that we are driving toward something at all times—social stability and social justice—and that we can therefore solve our own problems through the principle of social incorporation, that is, through making a place for everyone in society. But such social order and social ideals have too often blinded us to the reality of coercive forces in our everyday lives.

The equilibrium model cannot explain these forces as well as a point of view which would have us expecting *dis*equilibrium. Looking at society in this way creates expectations, not of social persistence and stability but of change; not of integration of structural elements through the operations of institutions by a consensus, but of conflict and dissensus; not of every social element in terms of its functional operation in creating or maintaining concensus, but of a view of each element contributing in some way to disintegration and change; and not in a sharing of values by all members but of an expectation of coercion by some of the others (Dahrendorf, 1959, pp. 161-63).

The existence of these two models is useful for analyzing the real social operations of any group. Even more important for our present concerns, the proposal of such a disequilibrium set of expectations allows us to see the discrepancy between the popular conceptions of our system and the divisive and discontinuous elements that exist within any community. This discrepancy between real and ideal is not a pattern to which just Americans, or Westerners in general, are subject. E. R. Leach points out the same popular concept of the social system among the Burmese Kachin, in the very book which most forcefully challenged the universal validity of the equilibrium model and showed the usefulness of the coercion set of expectations—*Political Systems of Highland Burma*: "This fictional procedure [of forcing data to conform to an equilibrium system] is not merely an analytical device of the social anthropologist, *it also corresponds to the way the Kachins themselves apprehend their own system** through the medium of verbal categories of their own language" (Leach, ix).

But not all peoples conceive of their lives in such terms of social balance. Some, rather, exhibit a vision of life in line with the model of disequilibrium. Such groups conceive of conflict as a norm, interpersonal and inter-group alienation as a probability in any given situation.

These observations apply, I believe, to lower-class blacks in the United States. Indeed, most American Negroes commonly conceive of life, I believe, in terms of a conflict model. At least, this set of expectations explains more of Negro attitudes and activities than does a world view which sees social life gravitating toward order and balance. And I believe that other studies of Negro communities bear this out. The most dramatic piece of evidence in this regard is to be found in Robin M. Williams' *Strangers Next Door*; he notes that "the most ubiquitous conception [held by] Negroes is that the white person is prejudiced against him" (Williams, p. 247). The interesting fact is that this is the *only* stereotypic feature that Williams reports that Negroes have of whites.** As opposed to the white stereotype of the Negro which focusses on a number of positively identifiable traits—such as animality, childishness, supersexuality—the reported Negro stereotype of whites is conceived not in terms of traits but rather attitude, and the attitude reacted to is one of animosity and fear leading inevitably to intergroup and interpersonal defensiveness and a vision of a life of perpetual conflicts.

The shock arising from the riots occurs because the white world,

---

* Italics added.

** This does not mean that Negroes have no similar stereotype traits for whites, but rather this is the one which probably can be elicited by whites as part of an on-going battle of wits which the questioner doesn't even know is taking place.

given its utopian bias, has always envisaged Negroes as part of a functioning and self-correcting social system, and the riots proclaim this vision to be in error. We have tried to defend a view that gives Negroes a "place" in the American social structure, but "place" implies a feeling that Negroes have never exhibited, for the most part, since the place accorded them was arrived at through coercion. For instance, in the South, we hear the rationale that Negroes are fine ("We love our Nigras") as long as they stay in their place, by which is meant social place, of course. A similarly coercive sense of place is announced in the North, but in geographical rather than social terms, whenever the Negro community is ghettoized. But the riots proclaim dramatically that such a sense of place has never been accepted nor prized; blacks may live in the ghetto, but there is little evidence that they like it there. It is now clear, because of the riots, that if balance or sense of place ever existed in Negro groups it was never achieved through a sharing of the white vision of life in idyllic and ordered terms. Rather, order has been established and maintained through coercion and constraint, through force imposed by one group upon the other. This dimension of constraint has been at the center of black-white relations since the introduction of the slavery system and may be regarded as the primary source of the disequilibrium model of life which Negroes hold.

> *Furthermore, this emphasis on a conflict-style of action is not solely focussed on the coercion imposed by the white man; it may be observed operating within Negro communities as well, especially in image-ideals of leadership and personal power. Those who conceive of themselves as in the midst of constant conflict can only imagine an organization in terms of personal power and interpersonal coercion, whether the power is imposed from someone within or outside the community.*

NAMING

Nowhere is the disparity between the white, balanced ("square"?) world view and the Negro conflict-oriented pattern more observable than in the different reactions to the "black power" movement. Most whites, including most liberals, begin to quake at the very mention of the term because it implies that power is more essential than innate justice in establishing identity, security, a sense of place in this country. This was clearly shown when liberal financial support was so quickly withdrawn when black power was first proclaimed. Furthermore, by talking in terms of *black* power, Negro militants were insisting on polarizing the world between blacks and whites, on setting parallel terms and concepts which emphasize this polar opposition.

The strategy of polarization is the diametrical opposite of that used by Negroes until recently. They took the compromising position in terms of the conflict; instead of insisting on being called "blacks" they argued that whites were not white at all but rather "pinko-gray." Thus, for a time the most common term for whites in Negro parlance was "gray." A parallel strategy was set forth by the proposal that middle-class Negroes be called "colored," or even better, "people of color," for dignity's sake. Now, by proposing "black" as their term for themselves, they turn their back on solutions of this sort.

A few years ago, Civil Rights workers took to calling Whitey "Chuck." The idea behind this was that in the South, one of the common terms for the white man was "Mr. Charley," a name stemming from the Southerner's insisting on the use of "Mr." before his name, as a mechanism for maintaining social distance and respect. When "Chuck" came into use, the humorous argument pursued was that "We used to have to call him 'Mr. Charley,' then someone called him 'Charley,' and before we knew it we were calling him 'Chuck.'" But black separatists have now gone one step further, and would insist that "*Mr.* Charles" is even more appropriate, thus reimposing the social distance, but on their own terms. Muhammed Ali has a system of addressing white men that underlines this approach:

> One of Clay's trademarks [is] calling white men by both their names. He likes to spot them approaching, and when they come into range, he beams and throws out with mock pomposity and careful syllabication: "An-ge-lo Dun-dee!" "Gor-don Da-vid-son!" "Gil-bert Ro-gin!" That is, if he remembers the name (Olsen, p. 19).

By espousing the term "black" for themselves, they are also arguing implicitly that "Negro" is a status term imposed by whites to underline the white's sense of the place of blacks in the American system, a sense which those who call themselves "black" no longer share.

This brings up the question of why expressions of this conflict-orientation have never before been forced on the consciousness of the complacent white world. But it has been a part of the white image and understanding for a long time, for Negroes have been conceived of in terms of constantly fighting, brutally killing each other, needing to be controlled because their animal passions might burst forth at any time. It is common knowledge that brutal behavior of black with black was countenanced by police and local law alike, and in certain ways openly encouraged. (The sordid scene in Ralph Ellison's *Invisible Man* of the staged black melee in the hero's youth is called to mind.) But until recently these conflict-motives have been successfully bottled up, directed inward on the Negro community itself. ("They're all right so long as they keep on killing *each other*.") The important change, then, brought about by the Civil Rights movement, has been the opportunity to direct the aggressions to the source of coercion—in a sense, fighting fire with fire.

LOOKING BACK

Negroes sensed this change-over in focus of aggression long before the Civil Rights movement, in fact as soon as the social effects of the northern migration were felt. This is reflected strongly in their folklore; there are many traditional stories which articulate the difference between Negro-white relations in the South and the North.

> This took place long many, many years ago before the Civil Rights Act. This Negro got on the train to Georgia and the porter came through and he says, "Boy, where's your ticket?" And the Negro showed him his ticket and of course when they got on up into South Carolina he came through he says, "Boy, let me see your ticket," and he gave him the ticket and of course when he got on into Virginia it was the same way, "all right Boy, get your ticket ready," and finally the train moved

on up across Mason Dixon line and the Porter came through he says, "Okay, Boy, I want to see that ticket again." The Negro jumped up and grabbed him by the collar; "Who are you callin' Boy?" [4]

There was this Negro who worked for, who was a porter or chauffeur, for this white man in South Carolina, and of course this white man was a segregationalist, and he was tired of all these Northern papers talking about what a hard time Negroes were having down in the South, so one day he called his chauffeur in, and he said, "Sam," he said, "are you satisfied with the way things are down here in South Carolina?" And Sam says, "Yes sir, boss, I'm satisfied." He said, "Well, you know I'm just so tired of all them Yankee radicals up there always talking about what you all want." He says, "I think I'll just pay for a television program and I want you to just go on the air and tell all them folks in New York, and Philadelphia, and Los Angeles, just how satisfied Negroes are down South." So Sam says, "Yes sir Boss." He said, "I'll go." He said, "All right then, we'll go tomorrow." So the next day he asked Sam about going, so Sam says, "Boss did you say that people, Negroes, everybody, were gonna hear me in New York, Los Angeles, and California, and Chicago?" He says, "Yes Sam." So when he got to the television station Sam says, "Boss, now you sure those people gonna hear me in New York, and Chicago, and Philadelphia," and he said, "Yes, Sam." He said, "Now Sam we're on the program." He says, "Here I have my chauffeur with me." Sam said, "Now you sure they gonna hear me boss," he whispered. He said, "Yes." He said, "Sam, I want you to just tell these people all over the country how satisfied Negroes are down here." Sam says, "Help, help!" [5]

LICENSE

The implication of this last story is that the aggressive pleas for help are always lying in readiness waiting for license for public pronouncement. This is a dimension of black attitudes toward aggression that cannot be ignored; frustrations will accumulate, looking for ways in which they can be given voice. What seems to characterize the ambience of Negro communities most fully in this realm is their constant readiness to give vent to their aggressions whenever and wherever the opportunity arises, and to see the expression as "entertainment" at the expense of the antagonists. So it is not just the tensions but the willingness—indeed eagerness—to express them in licentious and hostile terms. We can see just such a pattern operating in the riots.

> *There is a well-developed pattern of competitive expectations which prepares blacks, especially street-men, for aggressive activity wherever and whenever the chance arises.*

Furthermore, this kind of aggressive activity is a dimension of the play life of blacks, regarded by them as entertainment and therefore fully enjoyed because of the license to release otherwise pent-up emotions. In other words, not only are aggressions lying in readiness but preparations are made to capitalize on license whenever it arises, and a willingness is revealed to view any licentious and aggressive activity as entertaining communication. This spirit of readiness for license, aggression, and entertainment is the theme of many traditional stories such as the oft-repeated one concerning the Negro held back in life and what happened to him when he reached heaven.

two versions of a tale

One time an old religious man died and went to heaven. He lived in this world a good life. So Saint Peter saw fit for him to come up. He got up theah an he knocked on the doah. He say, "Saint Peter," say, "here I am. You sent for me." Said, "Yeaas." Said, "Now I'm here to get my wings." Saint Peter gave him a pair of wings an he began to fly around in the heavens and earth. All the other angels up there say, "Listen, let me tell you one thing. Brother, you bettah quit flying so fast. Say you might hurt yo'self." He say, "Well, I worked for 99 yeahs for these wings, and I'm gonna jest keep on flying." So he wuz a flying piece of furniture. He flew around and after a while he flew up 'side of a tree and broke one of his wings. I went over there and told him, I say, "Brother, I told you wuz gonna get hurt." He say, "Well," says,

"I'm glad I did. But I can tell you one thing, I sho' was a flying piece of furniture while I was flying'." [6]

This version of the story which comes from a very old Negro informant represents an older narrative tradition than most of the stories in this book. This story, however, has remained in the repertoire of black entertainers but with some important changes of focus, for heaven is seen to be segregated and the flying around therefore becomes a more overtly aggressive act.

This colored man died and went up there to meet his Maker. But when he got to the gates, St. Peter said that God wasn't home or having any visitors, by which he meant no Negroes allowed. Well this old boy, he had been a good man all his life and his preacher had told him that heaven would be his place, so he didn't exactly know what to do. So he just kind of hung around there, around the gates, until one time there St. Peter just had to go and take a pee. So while Pete was gone, this old boy slipped through, stole himself a pair of wings and he really took off. Sailed around the trees, in and out of those golden houses and all, swooped down and buzzed some of those singers and all, and had himself a good old time. Meanwhile, of course, St. Pete came back and found out what had happened and called out the heavenly police force to go get him. Well this guy was just getting the feel of wearing wings and he really took off, zoomed off. They had some little time bringing him down, him flying all over heaven fast as he could go. Finally they got him cornered and he racked-up on one of those trees, and I tell you, he looked like a mess with broken wings and all. So they took him and threw him out the gates, and there was one of his friends just coming up there. Says, "What happened, man?" Says, "Oh man, when I got here they wouldn't let me in to no white man's heaven, but I grabbed me some wings and I had me a fly." Says, "Oh yeah?" Man said, "Yeah, they may not let no colored folks in, but while I was there I was a flying fool." [7]

Between the generation of the first story teller and the second has come the increased opportunity through the migration northward; the adapted life style of the big cities has given rise to alternatives of licentious and competitive expressions which allow for more overt aggressive behavior with a clearer understanding of who the antagonists really are.

Clearly in the popular mind, it was the change of milieu and situation that allowed more overt aggressions and confrontations for Negroes. This change brought about a variation of attitudes toward aggression within the Negro community, a diversity mirrored in the various terms used by young Northerners for the practicers of the old Southern approach—"Uncle Tom," "Steppin Fetchit" and so on.

MEN-OF-WORDS

There are many ways in which Negro expressive culture reflects this conflict orientation. Reports of elaborate "cutting" or "jam" sessions in which musicians compete in musical terms are legion in writings on the roots of jazz, and similar contests can be observed between dancers, singing groups, even preachers. Words are especially valued as power devices, and men-of-words performers find ready audiences on street corners, in bars and pool halls, at parties, virtually wherever two or more people have congregated.

This kind of word show has often been witnessed by white observers, but seldom appreciated or understood because the recognition of beauty based on wit is something that whites do not fully share. A recent dramatic demonstration of just such an understanding gap arising from cultural disparity is to be found in the biography of Cassius Clay, *Black Is Best,* by the white sportswriter, Jack Olsen. In the first chapter, Olsen reports at great and fascinating length, a sample day's activities of the Muhammed Ali organization. Muhammed is surrounded by a chorus of amen-sayers and constantly holds forth for their benefit. He is a man-of-words of dimension and brilliance, but the nature of his rapport with his audience is missed by Olsen because of the culture gap. We read of Muhammed sermonizing in a preacher's voice, telling jokes, boasting, improvising a poem, narrating commentary for a film, singing, reminiscing, calling home, and generally keeping everyone entertained. Through all of this, Olsen patronizingly describes how Clay repeats himself, how he does not really extemporize poems but "repeats" ones made up for another occasion with the addition of only a few lines, how he turns every subject of conversation back on himself, and how completely and defensively self-centered the boxer is. But in spite of Olsen's moralizing, a picture of a powerful man-of-words in an oral culture shines through, a person capable of capturing and holding his audience's interest and admiration for days on end.

Another Negro man-of-words, Dick Gregory, has written his own story, and in this we get more of an inside view of such performers. He tells in various parts of the book how he developed his technique of humor through aggressive verbal contests. For instance, in his childhood he often found himself involved in contests of wit but seldom winning.

> I got picked on a lot around the neighborhood; skinniest kid on the block, the poorest, the one without a Daddy. I guess that's when I first began to learn about humor, the power of a joke.
>
> "Hey, Gregory."
>
> "Yeah."
>
> "Get your ass over here, I want to look at that shirt you're wearing."
>
> "Well, uh, Herman, I got to . . ."
>
> "What you think of that shirt he's wearin', York?"
>
> "That's no shirt, Herman, that's a tent for a picnic."
>
> "That your Daddy's shirt, Gregory?"
>
> "Well, uh . . ."
>
> "He ain't got no Daddy, Herman, that's a three-man shirt."
>
> "Three-man shirt?"
>
> "Him 'n' Garland 'n' Presley (his brothers) supposed to be wearing that shirt together."
>
> At first . . . I'd just get mad and run home and cry when the kids started. And then, I don't know just when, I started to figure it out. They were going to laugh anyway, but if I made the jokes they'd laugh with me instead of at me. I'd get the kids off my back, on my side. So I'd come off that porch talking about myself.
>
> "Hey, Gregory, get your ass over here. Want you to tell me and Herman how many kids sleep in your bed."
>
> "Googobs of kids in my bed, man, when I get up to pee middle of the night gotta leave a bookmark so I don't lose my place."
>
> Before they could get going, I'd knock it out first, fast, knock out those jokes so they wouldn't have time to set and climb all over me. . . .

And they started to come over and listen to me, they'd see me coming and crowd around me on the corner." *

With both Gregory and Muhammed Ali we see nearly all of the primary attributes of the man-of-words, the importance of inserting the performer in the midst of his performance, emphasized through the constant use of the first-person pronouns, the strong interaction between performer and audience, the identification of the performer with the item being performed, and most important, the development of performance technique in a contest atmosphere (Abrahams, 1964; 1968). This kind of self-deprecation, for instance, can become something of a boast in its use of hyperbole, and therefore the voicing of one humorous complaint can lead to a rejoinder and a casual remark becomes a battle of wits.

CONTESTS AND PLAYING THE DOZENS

I'm so broke, I couldn't buy a crippled crab a crutch if I had a forest of small trees.

Oh man, I'm so broke, I couldn't buy a dick a derby, and that's a small fit.

Yeah, well I'm so broke, I couldn't buy a mosquito a wrestling jacket, and *that's* a small fit.

My soles are so thin that if I stepped on a dime I could tell whether it's heads or tails.

I'm so hungry my backbone is almost shaking hands with my stomach.

I'm so hungry I could see a bow-legged biscuit walk a crooked mile.

I'm so broke, if they were selling Philadelphia for a penny, I'd have to run, afraid they would sell it to the wrong person. [8]

However, most contests of this sort do not generally turn back on the performer in this self-deprecating fashion. The boast is the norm,

* From the book *nigger: An Autobiography* by Dick Gregory with Robert Lipsyte. Copyright © 1964 by Dick Gregory Enterprises, Inc. Reprinted by permission of E. P. Dutton & Co., Inc.

and if deprecation is involved it is commonly directed at another. We can see this in a number of traditional verbal forms, perhaps most clearly in "playing the dozens." There are two ways of playing: the "clean dozens" and the "dirty dozens." The clean dozens commonly involve a series of clever insults:

> Now dig. Your house is so small, the roaches have to walk sideways through the hallways.
>
> Your mother is so small she can do chin-ups on the curb.
>
> Your mother is so fat, she has to have a shoehorn to get in the bathtub.
>
> Man, you're so dark, you need a license to drink white milk.
>
> If electricity was black, your mother would be a walking powerhouse.
>
> You look like death standing on a street corner eating lifesavers. [8]

In the clean dozens some of the insults are directed at the other's mother, but most are directly personal. On the other hand, in the dirty dozens, the mother of the other person is almost always the subject of the slur, and she is commonly subject to aspersions of illicit sexual activity, usually with the speaker. Thus, the dirty dozens involve insults that also serve as boasts. Commonly, the interplay begins with a simple curse, but soon turns into a *capping* session.

> 1. Fuck you, man.
> 2. Fuck your mama.
>
> 1. Fuck the one who fucked you.
> 2. Oh, man, go to hell.
>
> 1. Gi' your mama the key and tell her to come with me.
> 2. Your mama be there?
>
> 1. Dig man, wanna play the dozens!
>   I play Ringo Kid;
>   I fuck your mammy before your daddy did.
> 2. Your old lady look like the back of a donkey's ass.
>
> 1. I saw your mama in a swing;
>   Her pussy was shining like a diamond ring.

2. Look here, man, dig, let me get you straight;
   Your mammy got a pussy like a B-48.
   She's got somep'n between her legs call the "joo-jag-jam."
   It's hard to get, but it's good god damn!

1. At least my mom ain't cake—everybody get a piece.
2. Let me tell you somep'n.
   I fuck your mammy on a red hot heater;
   I miss her pussy and burn my peter. [8]

This rhymed way of playing the dirty dozens fills an extremely complex function in the development not only of men-of-words but of a sense of masculine identity for all youths who "play." The dozens provides the boy, who has commonly been raised in a matrifocal household, with a technique for "cutting the apron strings" by attacking another's mother knowing that his own mother will be attacked in turn (Abrahams, 1964, pp. 49–59). It also allows him practice in bringing aggressive language into artful form. This kind of verbal aggression is part of a larger system of "hidden language" which utilizes techniques of argument by indirection—called "signifying" in many black groups—which is tremendously important in the daily lives of lower-class Negroes.

> *But most important for our present concerns, playing the dozens provides, in expressive form, a statement of behavior conceived on a model of aggressive interpersonal activity but in a framework of useful and entertaining competition. The dozens can be viewed as the model of other verbal activities, for it presents a pattern of on-going, open-ended, competitive behavior which need not have a winner or a loser to justify the performance, since the competition is entertainment in itself. But because no winner and loser are declared,* there is a sense of the incomplete and the perpetual about this type of activity, when compared with white, middle-class expectations for such performances. We*

---

* It is not meant here that no one is considered the winner of such contests, for certain men-of-words are regarded as inevitable cappers. Their best caps are celebrated in their group in legendary stories. But each engagement is not ended with a declaration of winner or loser.

*expect a routine or story to have a beginning, middle, and
end, an expectation obviously not completely shared by Negro audiences. Furthermore, this pattern of on-going competition is observable in nearly all such activities, the most
obvious being the jam-session, for seldom do we have the
declaration there of winner and loser. Rather, competition
provides the atmosphere by which performers can best
perform.*

BEAUTIFUL PERFORMERS

The competitive frame of reference gives the performer a position
in black society which is extremely difficult for whites to understand.
Because such performers are able to assert their power confidently
and to embody it in such aggressive motives, they find an audience
which is willing to give its undivided attention for very long periods
of time. Furthermore, because the performer asserts hostility in a
world of license and gets away with it, he provides a model of behavior for all others who find themselves similarly coerced and
similarly conflict-minded. Consequently, the black audience thinks
of *performers* as "beautiful" as opposed to white use of the esthetic
term in reference not to the artist but to a work of art. In other
words, Negroes use the term in relation to good performers rather
than to effective performances. To call someone beautiful is not to
talk about physical characteristics so much as style, which means
primarily the ability to compete successfully in a hostile environment.

This use of "beautiful," an esthetic value word, is expanded then
into an ethical position. Those who can function well in handling
the recurrent problem of interpersonal or intergroup hostility are
conceived of as being successful in artistic terms. This use of "beautiful" is simply one example of the utilization of esthetic terminology
for ethical purposes.* "Jazzy," "Swinging," "Cool," "Soul," all derive
from emotional affect words from the good musical performance experience. All of them have been appropriated as descriptive of

---

* This is paralleled by the use of the word "ugly" meaning "bad" especially
in interpersonal situations.

personality, and all turn on a person's ability to handle recurrent problems through their exhibition of the proper style of toughness and resilience.

This is why those expressive performers who have been able to overcome the obstacles are "culture heroes" in a sense that no performer could ever be in the white world.* They have confidence in battle; they wear their warrior's image comfortably, something which not many blacks are able to do (Keil, p. 20). And if such performers combine ability with words with effective acts—as with Cassius Clay, Dick Gregory, Adam Clayton Powell, Willie Mays (at least early in his career), and "Sugar" Ray Robinson—then they assure themselves a place in the black pantheon. To be a hero, one must be willing to do battle for one's prestige, bully-style, to take on all comers at any time, to engage in an apparently never-ending series of conflicts.

TOASTS

This quality of enduring and eternal conflict is observable not only in the way in which the performers present themselves but also in the deeds of the heroes they celebrate. The never-ending battle is encountered and enjoyed by the central characters of those poetic improvisations called "toasts" or "toastēs" by street-corner talkers.

These epic fictions are performed in rhymed couplets, are commonly multi-episodic, and chronicle the deeds of various types of heroes.** Toasts are widely found among American Negroes, especially in the cities and in prisons. Many of them seem merely to present a central character in a series of situations in which he can show his abilities with words or actions. Seldom do his activities have the kind of dramatic climax we find in European literature;

---

* Conversely, villains' names such as "Uncle Tom" and "Steppin Fetchit" come from performers who don't act in the approved manner.

** I have described the presentation and compositional elements of toasts and printed a number of representative texts from South Philadelphia in *Deep Down in the Jungle*, pp. 99–173. See also Hughes and Bontemps (1959); Hughes (1966); Galoob (1963); Owens (1966). The techniques described by Olsen in his book on Cassius Clay make it obvious that Ali's poetizing is derived from toasting (pp. 7–10).

rather, he is presented as a "bully of the town" whose adversaries are numberless. This point is emphasized by the fact that in various tellings of these heroic toasts, incidents and confrontations are added and subtracted at will, and not just in the middle of the actions but also at the end. It is common, for instance, to tack on a visit to hell by the hero and a confrontation with the Devil and his family, such as we find in the toast about the only survivor from the wreck of the *Titanic*. This is made possible because of the improvised compositions of these poems in true epic style (Lord).

Shine and Stackolee

I don't know, but I think I will
Make my home in Jacksonville.
I don't know, but so they say,
The tenth of May was a hell of a day.
The captain and his mates were mumbling a few words
As the great *Titanic* knocked hell out of that first iceberg.
Up popped Shine from the decks below,
And said, "Captain, the water is at my boilerroom door."
He said, "Get, Shine, and do your act!
I've got forty-two pumps to keep the water back."
But before Shine could mumble another word
The great *Titanic* knocked hell out of that second iceberg.
Over went Shine and he began to swim,
Three thousand millionaires looking dead at him.
The Captain jumped up from the deck and called,
"Shine, oh Shine, please save poor me,
I'll make you richer than any Shine will ever want to be."
Shine said, "Your money is good as far as I can see,
But this ain't no shit for me.
There's whales in the ocean and there's fish in the sea,
Bring your red ass over and swim like me."
Up popped the millionaire's daughter upon the deck,
With her titties in her hand and her drawers around her neck.
She said, "Shine, oh Shine, please save my life;
On the tenth of May I'll be your lawful wedded wife."
He said, "I don't know, so I'm told,
The gals on the other shore has the same peehole.
The whales in the ocean are making it rough and tough,

And if I get to the other shore, it'll be damn good enough."
Shine swam for three days and three nights
When up popped the whale from the bottom of the sea,
And said, "You black motherfucker, you're trying to outswim me."
Shine said, "You swim good and you swim fast,
But you'll have to be a swimming motherfucker to catch my black ass."
When news got to Washington the great *Titanic* had sunk
Shine was on the corner of hun'ed and twenty-fifth street already half
  drunk.
At half-past four, Shine came in on the B and O,
And rolled up to the whore-house door.
And said, "Come here all you whores, and don't you pout,
Cause I'm a peter-pushing papa, and a water trout.
I measures thirty-six inches across the chest,
And I don't borrow nothing but sickness and death.
I've got a tombstone disposition and a graveyard mind.
I'm one motherfucker that don't mind dying."
When Shine was dead from drinking his gin,
The Devil said, "You're a long time coming, but you're welcome in."
He sent the Devil for a glass of water;
When the Devil came back he was fucking the Devil's daughter.
The Devil stooped over to pick up the glass;
He rammed his dick in the Devil's ass.
Two little imps standing against the wall,
Said, "Get that black motherfucker out of here before he fuck us all." [9]

Shine, in his abilities to engage in repartee in the midst of this trying situation, and in his apparently superhuman physical capacities, is a good representation of one type of Negro hero. But we are not given any feeling that his achievements in any of these arenas are permanent; rather we are left with the feeling that he must go on to further challenges, further victories.

This quality of being in perpetual conflict is also exhibited by the bad man, "Stackolee," in tales of his exploits. Stack doesn't have the resilience nor the sense of humor of Shine, but his abilities are no less pronounced.

> Back in '32 when the times was hard
> I carried a sawed-off shotgun and a crooked deck of cards.

Wore blue-suede shoes and carried a diamond can;
Had a six inch peck with a be-bop chain.
Had a one button robe and a lap-down hat;
And ever' time you saw me I looked just like that.
Well the times was gettin' hard and the weather was gettin' cold
My wife said, "Move on, motherfucker, your love's grown cold."
So I decided to take a walk down Rampart Street,
'Cause that's where I heard all them mean motherfuckers meet.
Well I waded through six inches of shit and ten inches of mud
And came upon a place called the "Bucket of Blood."
I told the bartender, "Give me sumpin' to eat."
He gave me a muddy glass of water and a tough piece of meat.
I said, "Look, son-of-a-bitch, you know who I am?"
He said, "Frankly, I don't give a damn."
I said, "Well motherfucker you better wake up and see
I'm that mean son-of-a-bitch they call 'Stackolee.' "
He said, "Yeah, I've heard of you from down the way
But I meet you motherfuckers 'most ever' day."
Well that's all he said, 'Cause he lay behind the bar with six holes in his
    head.
Bitch walked in said, "Bartender, if you please."
I say, "He lay behind the bar with six holes in his head."
She said, "I don't believe he's dead."
I said, "You can count the holes in his ragged-ass for yourself."
She said, "Better be gone when Billy Lyons comes back."
Spotted a bitch over at the next table
Rushed right over and grabbed me a seat
I said, "Hey baby, I don't wanna seem square
But who's this stud they call Billy?"
Well, she opened her pack [billfold] and pulled out a square [picture]
Said, "Well, he's tall, dark, and neat—
The meanest motherfucker on Rampart Street."
I could see she was stuck on this stud
So I said, "Move over baby, I'm laying you on the floor."
Bitch over at the next table smiled at me
I rushed right over and grabbed me a seat.
She said, "Hey, look like he ain't had any ass in quite a while"
I said, "Yeah, my wife threw me out
And I've been looking 'round for some other whore."
She looked at her watch, it said half past eight

Said, "Come upstairs and I'll set you straight."
When we got upstairs I threw her on the floor
I was anxious to get some ass off that frantic whore.
When we got back down to where we'd been before,
Well they was fucking on the tables, they was fucking on the floor.
In walked Billy Lyons.
He said, "Who might the murderer my good man be?"
I said, "It's me son-a-bitch, I'm Stackolee."
A punk jumped up, said "Go for the law."
Somebody hit that punk dead in the jaw.
Another punk went for the lights
But it was too late, I had Billy dead in my sights.
When the lights come on, Billy lay at rest
With a clip of my bullets dead in his chest.
Well we fucked all the whores, we drank the place dry;
I lay in the corner with blood in my eye.
Next morning when I woke I saw the judge and twelve good men
The judge said, "What might the charge on my good man be?"
Cop jumped up and said, "Rape, murder, and drunk in the first degree."
Bitch jumped up and started to shout.
Judge said, "Sit down motherfucker you don't know what it's all about.
Judge said, "Well, I'm gonna have to let you go, Stack,
'Cause I don't want to wake up with a knife in my back." [10]

Most toasts are concerned with heroes and therefore center on their series of victories. There is another and less common type, often found in prisons and hobo jungles, which tells more personal stories in episodic form and is suffused with the experience of defeat as part of the lesson of life. One such toast is "Toledo Slim."

Toledo Slim

Now this was down in old Joe's barroom, one cold December day,
We were just tell' jokes and funny stories just to pass the time away,
When the door came softly open and a form crept through the dim,
And all the boys stood around, for there stood Toledo Slim.
"How come Slim," said Boston Red, "You're looking on the bum?"
And all the boys stood around as Slim's story was begun.
He said, "Well, it's true boys, I'm on the bum—I'm on the bum for
   fair,

But in the past I lived 'em all, any door was always there.
I'd never turn a good friend down, I'd spend my money free,
And all the boys along the line were glad to stick with me.
But look here this all happened about five years ago, if I remember
     right;
I clipped a sucker for his roll, and popped clean out of sight.
So while riding around with the boys, we decided to get something to
     drink,
So we dropped in Kid McCoy's
And while I was sitting there, putting on a jolly and rollicky stew,
A dead-set Jane wandered in and sat beside me, too.
Wow, I asked if she'd have a drink and she politely said she would,
And as I gazed into her eyes I thought I understood.
And don't think I'm half drunk, boys, 'cause this isn't any dream,
'Cause when it came to pretty looks, this was a queen.
Now we chewed the rag for quite a bit and shot the corn for fair,
And when it comes to taking shuck, you can gamble I was there.
I told this broad here I'd place her in a finely furnished flat,
But when this joint closed up, I had this joint pat.
Now we searched the town looking for a pad.
And I paid a man's rent down
And she started working selling that body and soul and sure sewed up
     the town
And so then one night I had a job to do, the swellest place in town
So I packed my tools and started out with my pal sweet Jackie Brown.
Now this place was just a tumble, the one we done cased that night.
Everybody was sleeping. Wasn't a soul in sight
So we put the flag in a flash and started 'round the block,
But just as luck would have it we bumped into a cop.
So we dropped the flag quick as a flash and we run on down the street
But a bullet hit me in the leg and I knew I was beat.
Now a cop stopped and handcuffed me, but my pal he got away
And I didn't see his face again for many, many a day.
Now you all know what happened boys, they made quick work of me
They sent me up the river to do a little V.
But for them five years I didn't worry, them five years rolled away,
And I started back to Toledo town so happy and gay.
But when I got back to my flat I found my girl had done gone,
Gone with my pal sweet Jackie Brown and left me all alone.

So I searched the street both night and day, looking for my prey
And I swore I'd kill 'em both if it took to Judgment Day.
And then one day I met a wise guy, he knew my pal quite well,
Said he was livin' out in Frisco and doin' mighty swell.
But the girl now the girl died from T.B., so he said,
Died where my friend had left her for the want of the crust of bread.
Now all this happened cuttin' horse [heroin] and I didn't have a dime,
So I caught a West-bound freight-train with killing on my mind.
And then one foggy day on Market St. and in a sordid place
I ran across my friend Jackie and we stood there face to face.
And while we stood there staring I placed this luck on fate.
He tried to get the drop on me but was just a moment late.
And I sent a forty-five slug a crashing through his brain,
And during the excitement I caught an East-bound train.
So that's the end of my story boys that's why I'm just a bum.
I lost all ambition and don't care what I become.
But now you take heed to the story cause any dame most anywhere
can do the same to you.* [11]

This mood of resignation in the face of a competitive world is not characteristic of traditional fictions in active circulation in Negro communities today, especially in the cities. More characteristic are those that emphasize the bravado involved in the constant challenges of life, though the tone of resignation is still perceivable in certain lyric songs. In an earlier age, however, there were many illustrative stories pointing to wisdom to be gained from a defeating conflict experience, even if the lesson didn't carry with it the sorry-for-yourself point of view that the Toledo Slim toast does. Here, for instance, is a story in the Br'er Rabbit style which is still to be found in the repertoires of middle-aged raconteurs.

* It should be noted that the emotional focus of this piece and some of its cliches and conventions probably originated in hobo lore, and therefore is not to this extent Negro in origin; however, we are concerned here with Negro tradition, not necessarily Negro *invention*. Many, perhaps most of the items found in this work are part of an international fund of jest materials. Here the concern is to what uses these items have been put, and how their content reflects the perceptions, life style, and problems of black existence in the United States.

FROM AN OLDER MAN

Did you ever hear that one about that Rabbit and that Lion got to talkin' about who ruled the heaven and who ruled the earth. So the Rabbit told the Lion one time, says, "Brother Lion, if God rules the Heaven, man rules the earth." The Lion told him, "That's shit. God rule the Heaven and *I* rule the earth." Rabbit told the Lion, "I'll let you meet man." So that Sunday morning they went out. Rabbit went by and picked the Lion up, told him, "Come on and let's go meet man." You know. So they left going on down the road, and after awhile they met a little boy rolling a hoop along, you know. The Lion broke at him, you know. So the Rabbit told him, "No, no, Brother Lion, that *will* be man." "Goddamn, I thought that *was* man." So they went on up the road a little bit further, and there was an old fella cuttin' up wood on the wood pile with an axe. He broke at him. Rabbit said, "No, no," said, "That *have* been man." Went on down the road a little further, met a man on a horse, you know, with a Winchester rifle, a forty-five on his side, and a big bull-whip, you know. So the Rabbit said, "Now damn if that ain't man there." So the old Lion spared off and made a pass at him. That man was shootin' him in the face with that bull-whip, you know, and when he turned around he was shootin' him in the ass with that damn Winchester. That Rabbit asked that Lion, say, "Did you meet man?" He say, "You Goddamn right. I ain't never seen the lightning so fast in my face and thunder in my ass in all my damn life." He said, "If you think that I'm lyin', take a glimpse at my ass when I pass." [12]

This is a parable of accommodation, not the sort of story which one therefore finds among the young men; but, like the newer stories, it talks in terms of learning to live with fear and of defining one's relations with others in terms of power. And the focus of this power is explained somewhat in the story of Lion, Rabbit, and Man, by the fact that "the man" is an expression meaning "white-man boss," and the description of him makes him sound like the overseer or the prison guard. But there has been a changing attitude toward fictional opponents especially when they are white, so the accommodating pose is no longer regarded as viable, and those who use this approach are called "rag-heads" and "Uncle Toms."

DISTRUST

One of the deep-seated characteristics exhibited in these stories, and emerging from the frame of reference in which conflict and coercion are the norms, is the active distrust of others that these fictions preach. This feature suffuses Negro traditional expression and, in a manner of speaking, will provide some of the major subjects of this study. Lion learns not only not to trust Man, but also not to rely on Rabbit or anyone else with whom he may argue.

This distrust of even one's closest friends is a constant theme of Negro life and Negro fictions. We see this in the earliest reportings of traditional narratives; in fact, one of the most salient features of the talking animal story is what one might call a "pattern of progressive dissolution of friendship." This pattern derives from African sources where there are indications that these stories serve as cautionary tales on how an antinormative, asocial, childlike creature can work to upset friendships. But in an atmosphere of distrust, these stories serve in a more illustrative fashion, explaining why, when everyone is looking out for his own childish interests, one can not trust anyone. These stories, in the United States, seem to talk about the Br'er Rabbits all around us.

Brother Rabbit and Brother Terr'pin

This is a story about Brother Rabbit. There are different types of animals in the woods. They—him and Brother Terr'pin—were cuttin' buddies. It comes drought one time. And they was both thirsty—just all the water they could get was off the grass in the morning—it was so dry for dew. And it got so bad then. The grass got so short they couldn't make it at that. So they finally had to talk it over with one another. So Brother Rabbit says to Brother Terr'pin, says, Brother Terr'pin, we been trying to make it; we can't find no water. Says, you're so slow. Say, you just stay here and let me run off out here in the woods. Some way I'll try and locate some water. And I'll come back and get you. So Brother Rabbit, he leaves Brother Terr'pin and he come across an old house and one of these old cisterns—old two bucket cisterns—one bucket up and one bucket down. Well, one was down and one was up. Well the one that was down was just sitting on the water. There wasn't no water in it and the other was just hanging. So Brother Rabbit hopped up on that little boxed in part. You know. They got this cistern and he could smell where this bucket had been wet and he hopped in this bucket what was up and went down and the other bucket came up. Well that let Brother Rabbit down there in the well. Well, he got him plenty of water and he got full and he just stayed there in that bucket in that well. So, along one day come Brother Terr'pin. He finally made it. He mighty slow and he hopped up on this boxed in part they had around the cistern of the well and he looked down in the well and he seen all that water down in there and he says, Brother Rabbit, say is that you? He says, yes, says I'm down here and I'm full a water and it's cool and I sure wish you could get some. Says, tell you what, says, hop in that bucket and come on down. So Brother Terr'pin gets in this other bucket and it goes down. Brother Rabbit comes up. Brother Rabbit got to the top of the cistern and he hops out of his bucket and jumps over on the side of the well and sits there and watches Brother Terr'pin drink. He drink and he drink and he drink. So Brother Rabbit asked him, says, how's it down there Brother Terr'pin? Says, it's fine. I'm full of water and I ready to come up. He says, I'll tell you what. He says, What is it. He says I'm gonna hop off out here in the woods and then I'm gonna be seeing you. So he says—Oh, Brother Rabbit, you ain't gonna go off and leave me down in this well, is you? He says, That's the way the world's going now. Some up and some down. [13]

Significantly, "up" and "down" are the very terms used in black street parlance for the outcome of the verbal contest. "Down" means to place someone at a disadvantage. One can "down" someone or "put down" someone, or one can "get up on" someone. Capitalizing on the sexual implications of the up-down contrast, another term for verbally besting is "mounting." Mounting and putting someone down are, of course, consonant with the aggressive contest orientation of the streets, and the existence of this terminology emphasizes the preparation everyone (at least all the men) must go through to handle the repeated life battles, to learn to fight back and enjoy it.

However, fashions of fighting back and modes of enjoyment and endurance have changed as Negroes have adapted to different geographical and social circumstances. The device of winning contests through guile, as does Br'er Rabbit, has been rejected by many Negroes; this is especially true of large segments of young black men in the cities, who would rather engage in contests of power than to aggress with the wits. A clear statement of this rejection emerges in the one Br'er Rabbit story which I collected from a young man.

FROM A YOUNGER MAN

Brother Fox had been trying to get Brother Rabbit for a long time. So he told Brother Bear one day, he said, "Brother Bear, now I know how we can trick that old rabbit into giving himself up." Brother Bear said, "How will we do it?" He said, "Now we'll invite all the animals in the forest to a party, all except Brother Rabbit. He'll be so embarrassed and hurt that he won't want to live and he'll give himself up. And we'll have rabbit stew before the week is up."

So all the invitations were around. So that Saturday evening, you know, all the animals were going down to the party. Even the skunk washed up and put the perfume on, went into the party. Brother Rabbit was sitting on the post and all. Said, "Where you all going?" "Down to Brother Buzzard's house." "Brother Buzzard?" "Yeah. Brother Fox is giving a party over there." Rabbit ran to the house and got dressed, and ran down to the house. Brother Buzzard said, "Sorry, Brother Fox and Brother Bear say they don't want you in it. I'm sorry, that's what they told me."

So the Rabbit turned away with his head turned down. He feeling sad, downhearted, tears in his eyes. Felt like he was alone in the world. But then he got mad. He said, "I know what I'll do." He went home and shined his shoes, and got his shotgun and went back and kicked the door open. "Don't a motherfucker move." He walked over the table, got all he wanted to eat. Walked over to the bar and got himself all he wanted to drink. He reached over and he grabbed the Lion's wife and he danced with her. Grabbed the Ape's wife and did it to her. Then he shit in the middle of the floor and he walked out.

So after he left, you know, the Giraffe jumped up. He said, "Who was that little long-eared, fuzzy-tailed motherfucker just walked in here with all that loud noise?" The Bear looked at him and said, "Now look, no use getting loud. You was here when he was here, why didn't you ask then?" (Like guys, they like that. You always get bad after the other person is gone, but you never say nothing while they is there.) [14]

This story says, by implication, that the old ways of Rabbit no longer work; only the assertion of power with devices like a gun will answer the problems of conflict. Furthermore, Rabbit specifically attacks here the problem of social exclusion; his answer to the challenge posed by being ostracized is not only to fight back but to exercise power, to seize the very features of life denied him, and to thumb his nose as he does so. This solution to recurrent social problems is offered both in regard to intra- and inner-group conflicts; this can be seen both in everyday life situations and in those portrayed in traditional fictions.

BLUES POWER

During the riots in Washington, D. C. that followed the assassination of Martin Luther King, Jr., the authorities looked around for a Negro figure that the majority of rioters—the street-men—would listen to. The man that they came to choose was not a political leader, nor the head of a civil rights organization, but a singer, James Brown, "Soul Brother No. 1." The *Washington Post* reported that "The move to get him here began when . . . a troubleshooter for Mayor Walter E. Washington asked Petey Green for advice. . . . Green, a 38-year-old ex-convict and narcotics addict immediately suggested the 'soul singer.' Brown's plea was characteristically black, in rhyme, witty, pointed, aggressive. 'Don't terrorize—organize! Don't burn—Give the kids a chance to learn. Go home . . . Listen to the radio. Listen to some James Brown records . . . [I] Used to shine shoes in front of a radio station in Augusta, Georgia. Today I own that station. . . . That's black power—own something, be somebody.' "

That this singer was called upon in such a crisis underlines the point that entertainers fill a different position in black society than in white; they are regarded as power figures because of their abilities to generate and dominate an entertaining conflict, to control an audience, to get others to identify with them. This audience attitude has been reinforced because entertainers are allowed to live in the style most approved by black street-men, and they can do so with virtual impunity, for even white audiences admire flamboyance in entertainers. Furthermore, performing has been one of the few ways in which a black person has been able to live in such style without appearing to be a deviant or a criminal. Consequently, the black entertainer—especially the singer—has come to regard himself as the model of Negro life and to bring black values and aspirations into his performances.

In a much fuller way than in white popular music, black songs have involved themselves with the details of day-to-day black existence. Paul Oliver, in his remarkable work *Blues Fell This Morning* (1960), documents this in regard to the song of the era 1900–1945. He shows how the problems of finding work, keeping it, getting along with the boss, the best friend, the "old lady" (woman being lived with), and the necessity to keep travelling suffused the compositions of the street-corner bluesman. In fact, the blues singer came to be the model of the wandering class* of workers who populated the turpentine and lumber camps, who worked building the railroads, who drifted northward becoming the first wave of the ghetto-dwelling men.

The word "blues" came to characterize the compositions of these singers, blues being the sense of alienation or psychological isolation in which life becomes unbearably anxious, and communication becomes impossible. Leadbelly said something of this when he remarked that:

> All negroes like blues. Why? Because they were born with the blues.
> . . . When you lay down at night, turn from one side of the bed all night to the other, and can't sleep, what the matter? Blues got you. Or when you get up in the morning, and sit on the side of the bed—may have a mother or father, sister or brother, a boy friend or girl friend, or husband or a wife around—you don't want no talk out of any of um. They ain't done you nothing—but what's the matter? Blues got you. Well you get up and shev your feet down under the table and look down in your place—may have chicken and rice, take my egvice, you walk away and shake your head, you say "Lord have mercy. I can't eat and I can't sleep." What's the matter? Why the blues still got you (Ramsey).

However, where the blues as a feeling makes communication impossible, in the hands of a bluesman the feeling is converted into

---

* This was recognized by a number of white observers, notably Howard Odum, in his books about "Black Ulysses," and Roark Bradford.

the occasion for a song, and as a song it acts therapeutically to both the singer and his audience. As one singer put it:

> When I have trouble, blues is the only thing that helps me . . . I mean that's the only way to kind of ease my situation. If I have lots of troubles, for instance, rent situation, and so forth and so on like that, the blues the only thing that gives me consolation (Lomax).

It is this ability to capitalize upon an adverse state and to develop it into a creative form that propels the performer into the position of leadership. He makes himself seem bigger than life by taking life's adversities and using them, controlling them in his play world of art, making a victory out of what seemed like a defeat.

In this the singer is aided greatly by his willingness to identify himself strongly with his compositions. He gives the impression that he is living this common experience, just as his audience has, but he has been able to use the situation for creative purposes. He is the controller, the manipulator, his audience the controlled and the coerced. Thus in a very real sense he is the hero of the group because he is a battler and a winner. When his music is blue it is because his audience is rootless and unsatisfied and lonely too. When "soul" becomes possible, it is he who gives it its most characteristic expression, pointing to the way things are in a world filled with interpersonal tensions but in which more stable relationships have become a possibility.

3

Down South, during slavery there was this Negro who would ask for everything that no one else wanted. So that went on for a long time, and finally the slaves were set free, and the owner of this Negro called John gave a big feast in his honor. So in order to break him of this habit of always wanting everything and asking for it, the Master gave a big feast. They had food spread out all over the place and that's all John could see—food everywhere he looked. So just while they were saying their blessing, everyone said their blessing, but old Master and he was last. And he said, "The Lord is my shepherd, I shall not want," and John said, "Well, give it to me, then." [15]

One of the greatest areas of misunderstanding between whites and blacks is in the nature of the ghettoes and the meaning of living there. Given their orientation of "place," whites see it as home for Negroes, never recognizing that to most blacks the concept of "home" is almost meaningless because of their transitory existence. Residence in one place over a number of years is exceptional for any but those matriarchs whose children provide them with the wherewithal to stay in one place. For the others, it is a constant battle of wits between pursuing slum landlords and evading tenants. Not only is income low, but rents are high, forcing slum-dwellers to pay an excessively high proportion of income on rent and to move whenever they get too far behind in rental payments (U. S. Riots Commission, pp. 470–2). Consequently, little sense of neighborhood and of pride in living quarters is established or establishable. The riots, when they focussed on the ghettoes themselves (rather than on what whites feared most, the suburbs) were announcing this emotional dissatisfaction. As the Riots Commission succinctly put it: "What white Americans have never fully understood—but what the Negro can never forget—is that white society is deeply implicated in the ghetto. *White institutions created it, white institutions maintain it, and white society condones it.*" (U. S. Riots Commission, p. vii) So when ghettoes are burned and pillaged, a comment is being made about living there.

RIOT

That this is not understood by whites is clear, for discussions of the riots almost always turn to some expression of *what Negroes are doing to themselves.* A recurring note in some of these conversations is that the rioters are playing right into the hands of the bigots by conforming to the stereotype of being irrational and destructive and falling to thievery. There can be little argument against this, because thievery and destruction do occur. The riots are simply announcing to the white world that it may think that life in the ghettoes has changed, because of recent legal decisions and government actions, but it hasn't. Ghetto Negroes are beset with the same economic, social, and psychological problems as before. The only changes that have occurred are in the extent of hope and the depth of frustration and the intensified feeling of distrust of blacks for whites.

The riots are not revolutionary; they put no program into effect and they exhibit only a spasmodic plan of attack. They do publicly proclaim, however, that the American Dream is still being pursued, and still being frustrated. Stokely Carmichael says just this in his book *Black Power*: "In America we judge by American standards, and by this yardstick we find the black man lives in incredibly inadequate housing . . . in segregated neighborhoods and with this comes *de facto* segregated schooling, which means poor education, which leads in turn to ill-paying jobs." (Carmichael and Hamilton, pp. 155–156.) And this is the essential "message" of the riots. As

Robert Fogelson, an historian of the riots, points out: "Far from rejecting the national ideology, the rioters demanded that all citizens fully honor it; they insisted on changes in practice, not principles. . . . The rioters made it clear to reporters during the riots and to interviewers afterwards that they expected the rioting to improve their position by arousing white concern. They could not know then —and indeed they may not know now—that, if anything, the whites, though more concerned, are also more intransigent. Put bluntly, the Negroes delivered a protest, but the whites did not hear it." (Fogelson, p. 16)

Most whites did not read the message clearly because in rioting the Ghetto Negro acted in a manner which whites were able to categorize as typical. Whites viewed these acts of protest as further examples of the disorganized, dishonest, and immoral life style of the blacks.

IMAGE

How did the rioters get caught in this misunderstanding of motive? The answer to this lies in the ambivalent image of themselves that Negroes have developed under the stern tutelage of whites. The slaves, once deculturated, were provided with a stereotype of themselves that they learned to accept (or "accommodate"). At the same time, however, the slaves developed a mechanism of fighting back; though they accommodated the stereotype image, they converted their supposed animality, supersexuality, and childishness, even thievery, laziness, and strong smell, from negative to positive attributes. Thus blacks have been able to use the stereotype as an aggressive weapon against the very society which imposed it. This has been one of their primary means of giving voice to this conflict.

This operation is costly, however, for it still adds up to an acceptance of the white stereotype. There must be an ambivalence about conforming to the stereotype since both the white world and important segments of the Negro community continue to regard them as negative. Furthermore, the acceptance and conversion of the traits leads to activities and attitudes which are uncreative and unfulfilling, indeed noticeably destructive and, all too often, suicidal.

The destructive activities of the riots are similar to those portrayed as "heroic" in many Negro traditional narratives. In a very real sense these fictions are related to the actions for they have been one of the primary devices by which the Negro self-image has been formulated, transmitted, and maintained. But the heroic image has, in great part, been fabricated out of traits imposed upon the Negroes in negative ways by the assuredly nonheroic white world.

ACCOMMODATION

This chapter will be concerned primarily with how these traits became accepted and in what ways they have been used by blacks, both in their oral literature and in their more overt expressions. We are dwelling here in the realm of what John Dollard has called the "Lore of Accommodation."

> Accommodation attitudes are those which enable the Negro to adjust and survive in the caste situation as it is presented to him. Originally the alternatives to accommodation were successful conflict with whites or extinction. There was little prospect of success in conflict . . . so the only possible alternative was adjustment to the situation. . . .
>
> Accommodation involves the renunciation of protest or aggression against undesirable conditions of life and the organization of the character so that protest does not appear, but acceptance does. It may come to pass in the end that one identifies with it and takes it into the personality; it sometimes even happens that what is at first resented and feared is finally loved (Dollard, pp. 250, 255).

The theory of accommodation is an extremely attractive one for an understanding of black-white relations, especially in regard to the amazing conformation of Negro personality types to certain of the stereotype trait-clusters. The theory is so attractive, in fact, that Stanley M. Elkins devoted a large section of his book *Slavery* to an exploration of the psychological dimension of the accommodation pattern. But Elkins' point of view is almost as ignorant as Dollard's of the defensive-aggressive direction that apparent accommodation features may take. Only in a footnote does Elkins acknowledge that subservience may be used as an aggressive weapon, and he was driven to this on the suggestions of the psychoanalyst, Bruno Bettelheim. Elkins notes: "This involves the principle of how the powerless can manipulate the powerful through aggressive stupidity, literal mindedness, servile fawning and irresponsibility." (Elkins, pp. 132–33n) He might have added to this repertoire of aggressive-defensive traits most of the others in the Negro stereotype—thievery, sexual abandon, childishness, and so on.

AGGRESSION

The use of these traits for aggressive purposes has a certain irony to it, and does permit hostility directed toward the very source of the group's greatest frustrations. But the ego-gains derived from such activities are small and short-lived because they do not generally register any reaction in the white world. Even though the traits are converted, the argument is still being waged on white man's terms. The actors exhibiting the traits continue to function as miscreants, not only in the eyes of the white world, but also in those of the preachers and matriarchs within the Negro community.* Furthermore, the aggressions allow little of the long-term gains needed to build a stable and meaningful self-image; it is difficult to embody such an image in negations. The aggressions only seem to be directed at the white world alone; given their continuing negative associations, even in the minds of the aggressors, the acts become in part self-castigating. The rhetoric of the actions is a confused one, for they seem to say two contradictory things at the same time: "Look how big, brave, and dangerous I am," and "Look how degraded and worthless I am." No wonder their message calling for recognition and power, when expressed in terms of riots, is misunderstood.

This self-defeating aggression pattern seems to have arisen early in the New World Negro experience. In the activities and fictions of

---

* The argument here never presupposes any uniformity in attitudes throughout American black communities, only a uniformity of social situation and a consequent sharing of ways of handling it. The lack of community agreement is explained, in part, by the divisions explored in Chapter Five.

the Ante-bellum and Reconstruction periods, the traits of the stereo-type converted were those which could be expressed most easily in a covert way: laziness, childishness, irrational beliefs, and "misuse" of language. In the 40's and 50's, more active though still covert activities, such as "Pushin' Day," developed. In this, Negroes took off from work and went to the most crowded stores in town to do some "pushin'" which can be done without much fear of arousing attention or reprisal. More recently this type of aggressive activity has been more overt, in sit-ins, marches, and riots. This changing approach to the problem is strongly reflected in their traditional narratives as well.

MARSTER-JOHN TALES

The two types of stories of greatest currency in Negro groups, urban and rural, have been trickster tales and jokes. These humorous story-types are aggressive in their conception and allow the storyteller and his audience to channel frustrations with greatest economy. At one time, tales of trickster in the guise of Br'er Rabbit were quite common. In these, as in the "Lion-meets-Man tale," Rabbit goes through a series of adventures in which he is able to dupe the animals larger and more powerful than himself. To get away with his tricks, Rabbit must not only have audacity and drive, but also the self-serving purpose and direct expression of hungers, characteristic of the child. And it is in the guise of the childish creature who really cannot be held accountable for his actions that we commonly observe and judge Rabbit. This childish behavior and approach to life is, of course, one of the major characteristics imputed to the Negro.

This conversion technique is even clearer in the nonanimal trickster tales in currency since Emancipation. The most widely-found trickster of this class is the slave John (or Tom, Sam, or Efan), who crops up in many stories in direct confrontation with his "ol' Marster." Though in some tales Marster outwits John, it is often at Marster's expense as well; and in most cases, John and Marster team up against the other whites or John clearly gets the better of his owner. The most common type is where John is able, sometimes in-

advertently, to get out of a tight spot which he has gotten into because of being stereotyped (and living up to one or another trait)
by an act which is at one and the same time an act of submission and
aggression. The hostility is usually blunted because Marster finds
John out, but it is there nonetheless. This is true, for instance, of the
most widely-found of the Marster-John stories, "The Coon in the
Box."

> This here fellow was working on a farm. Colored fellow. One night
> they was sitting outside, boss said, "Sam, what's that there behind that
> log?" "I can't see it, boss." He said, "Well, there's a rumor going
> 'round that you are psychic." He said, "Well, I gather that it's nothing
> but an old rabbit down there." So they went down and they took a peek
> and it was a rabbit. Said, "What's that behind the tree there?" Sam
> looked at the tree. "I can't see it, I guess it ain't nothing but an old
> squirrel. Maybe a black snake done got it." They looked around there
> and a black snake had bit the squirrel.
>
> White man looked and said, "If Sam is psychic, I'ma make some
> money off of that." So he said, "Sam, I'ma get all the people out here
> and next week we gonna get something, and you gonna tell us what it
> is."
>
> So the white man went and bet up all his property, saying Sam could
> tell them anything they want. So the one guy, he betted him. He said,
> "I tell you what. I know things you can't guess." So he went down got
> a steel box, then he caught a buzzard. They put the buzzard under the
> box.
>
> So the white man said, "In the morning, Sam you got to tell us what's
> in that box, or my land's up against it." Sam said, "All right, boss."
> But Sam knew he wasn't psychic, he was just guessing. He eased out of
> the house 'bout four o'clock in the morning, went and peeped under the
> box. Then he went back to bed. That morning he woke up 'bout ten
> o'clock. Sam come on out. "What's in the box there, Sam?" Sam said,
> "Hmm, I don't know. Lord, let me see now. Size of the box, I guess you
> got a buzzard under there." "Sure is. Sure is psychic, ain't he?"
>
> Guy said, "I'ma get you. Next week I'ma get you. Next week I'ma
> put something under that box, see if you guess it." "All right, captain."
> So the next Friday night, came out, put a coon under the box. Sam got
> up 'bout four o'clock, eased out of the house. The guy had two
> policemen sitting on the box. Sam couldn't see what was under that one.

Sam went back in the house, back to bed. White man came 'round, said, "Sam, if you don't win this morning, I'm broke. Out of business. I'm ruined. And if you don't say what's under that box tomorrow," he said, "you just one hung child." Now Sam was scared.

So morning came, they woke Sam up, 'bout ten o'clock. Sam came outside, he scratched his head, he looked at the box, looked at the people. Guy whispered to his friend, "He'll never guess there's a coon under there." Sam said, "Well, captain, you all finally got the old coon." So he went free just by saying that. [16]

This story emphasizes, through the punch-line, that John is to be regarded as a representative Negro in conflict with the white world. And his activity is once again directly related to a facet of the Negro stereotype—in this case, the propensity of the Negro toward childish belief in various kinds of occult powers. Here Sam, who knows he isn't psychic, is able to capitalize upon the trait by appearing to capitulate to it. The ironic approach, however, blunts the force of the aggression.

This ironic transformation of stereotype is true of virtually every trait of this sort. Laziness, stupidity, and thievery are all constant themes of the Marster-John cycle, devices used by John as a means of getting the better of Marster. Richard M. Dorson records a number of stories, for instance, in which John becomes a thief and has to talk his way out of punishment when caught. (John's trickery is usually expressed verbally.)

John stole a pig from Old Marsa. He was on his way home with him and his Old Marsa seen him. After John got home he looked out and seen his Old Marsa coming down to the house. So he put this pig in a cradle they used to rock the babies in in them days (some people called them cribs), and he covered him up. When his Old Marster come in John was sitting there rocking him.

Old Marster says, "What's the matter with the baby, John?" "The baby got the measles." "I want to see him." John said, "Well, you can't; the doctor said if you uncover him the measles will go back in on him and kill him." So his Old Marster said, "It doesn't matter; I want to see him, John." He reached down to uncover him.

John said, "If that baby is turned to a pig now, don't blame me" (Dorson, pp. 137–138).*

Another common theme might be termed "competitive laziness":

> Once there were three white slave owners sitting around discussing how lazy their slaves were. Each had one slave they said was the laziest man alive, so they decided to make a bet. So the first took them to his place and pointed to this man out in the fields sleeping. He said, "Man, couldn't nobody's nigger be any lazier than mine, 'cause my nigger is so lazy he lays in the field all day and lets flies swarm over him and snakes crawl on him and he won't move." So they went to the next place, the next man pointed out this slave, and said, "Your slave ain't nothing. You see that one, I saw him the other day in the cotton field and a cow came by and just shit and pissed all in his face and he didn't move." Now John really was the laziest, but he was all the time putting it over on Marster. But this was one time Marster didn't mind, 'cause when they went over to that place, John knew they were coming and what for and he just lay there on the ground moaning. Marster said, "Y'all ain't heard nothing yet. You see John there; well yesterday I heard moans and groans coming from the barn and I went out to see what was wrong. There the nigger was, lying in the corner moaning and groaning. You know what was wrong? He was lyin' on his nuts and was too lazy to move." That was what John told him, and that's why Marster won that bet. [17]

Another on the same theme has John aggressing through laziness and through taking advantage of Marster's good humor. In the end, John is forced back into line because of Marster's powers and wit, but not until he has thoroughly enjoyed himself at Marster's expense.

> Well, once upon a time there was a boss man had a laborer named John. John was a spook [Negro]. So John did all the boss man's work, worked hard day in and day out, night and day, worked hard all the time. Boss man figured John needed a vacation. So he said, "John, I'm gonna tell you what, boy." "What is it?" "Look, I'm gonna pay your way

* Reprinted from *American Negro Folktales*, compiled by Richard M. Dorson, by permission of Premier Books, Fawcett Publications, Inc. Copyright © 1956, 1967 by Richard Mercer Dorson, and 1958 by Indiana University Press.

to anywhere you want to go, for as long as you want to, just 'cause you've been so good to me." John said, "Yes sir, yes sir, boss, yes sir, what I been needing, what I been needing!" "Yeah, I figure you been needing one, too. So that's what I'm gonna do."

So John packed up his bags and tore ass the next day. So first he said, "I been hearing so much about New York City, I'm gonna check that out first." You see John was from the South, down in Louisiana or one of those foreign countries down there. Then he went to New York City, stayed there and partied for about two or three days. His boss man had given him two or three hundred dollars when he left. Well, John had done popped that money in three days. He sent back: "Boss man, I ran into my mother and my little baby sister was sick and I had to spend some money and I ain't got no money. You better wire me a hundred dollars." The boss man took a hundred dollars and wired it to him.

Well, John partied some more. The next couple of days he sent back and told the boss man he had met his wife and she had had another baby and he need some dust [money] to get her out of the hospital. The boss man sent him another telegram. "John, here's another hundred dollars." So John kept that shit up about five or six weeks while he was gone.

Then the boss man said, "I'm getting sick of this black-ass nigger telling me to send him all this money back. I know what I'm going to do. I'm going to send him something." So the boss man went down to the telegraph office and asked the man for a telegram. The office attendant said, "Look. Say, Mister, what you want on it." The boss man said, "Just write down there six m's and an f. He'll know what I'm saying." John was laying dead waiting to get some more money in a telegram. John got it, opened it up, read it and said, "Umm, guess I better get on home. Six m's and an f. You! Meet my mule Monday morning, mother-fucker." [17]

But the most aggressive type of Marster-John story is that in which John actually gets the better of Marster and in the process causes him to appear ridiculous. This type, which is still abundantly evident in Negro repertoires, commonly turns on some kind of obscene reference in which Marster commits an act of aggression which is turned back on him by the clever slave, often at the expense of both Marster's pride and his masculine image.

There once was a Negro slave named Tom who was so smart that his Master told everyone in town not to make any bets with him. It so happened that another white man in town wanted to buy Tom. So the original Master told him, "O. K., I'll let you buy Tom, but I must warn you never to make a bet with him." So the white man said, "Oh, I'm smarter than a nigger anyday." He bought Tom and just as sure as life, Tom shortly thereafter propositioned the man. He said, "Master, I'll bet you anything that you're constipated." The white man said, "What? No, I'm not. I know I'm not constipated." Tom said, "Well, if you're not constipated I'll bet you a thousand dollars that by twelve o'clock you will be." So his Master said, "All right, you've got a bet."

At twelve o'clock Tom came back. He told his Master that he had to test to see if he was constipated. The Master asked, "How do you do this?" Tom explained that he would have to pull down his pants and let him stick his finger up his ass. The Master agreed to this. Tom did it, and said, "Well, you're not constipated." Master said, "Well, I guess that means you owe me a thousand dollars." Tom said, "All right." The Master went off happy because he had won the bet and outsmarted Tom. He happened to be bragging to a friend about this and his friend said, "What? Man, Tom had bet me two thousand dollars that by twelve o'clock today he'd have his finger up your ass." [18]

———

There was this nigger down South who was working on a large plantation during slavery time. So every Thanksgiving vacation his boss would think of some kind of new thing to put over to get enjoyment. So it was getting closer and closer to Thanksgiving and the boss hadn't thought of anything exciting to do. So he saw John out by the barn one morning and told John, he said, "Whatever you do to that turkey, we are going to do it to you." So John went to bed that night and he couldn't hardly sleep thinking that if he cut the turkey's throat they would cut his throat, if he shot the turkey they would shoot him, if he hung the turkey they would hang him. He had to think of something quick because the time was nearing and he didn't have any to waste. So finally John thought over all of the possible fates that he would have if he did not do the right thing to the turkey. The next morning all the white folks were gathered around John and the turkey awaiting his decision because they know whatever John did to the turkey they would have to do it to him. So with pressure on him from both sides he came across a splendid idea. He caught the turkey, looked at it close, and turned the ass-end around and kissed the turkey's ass. All at the same time, he pulled down his pants and said, "Come on, white folks, don't rush yourselves, I've got plenty of it here." [19]

WHITE MAN, NEGRO, MEXICAN

Just this kind of aggression is directed against the white man in another widely-found series of stories centering on "White man, Nigger, and Jew" or in Texas, more commonly "White man, Negro, and Mexican." These are Negro versions of the international type of jest that plays off the cultural traits of three or four different ethnic groups or nationalities (American, British, French, for instance) with the intent of illustrating the superiority of one's own group.

These stories focus on stereotypical traits, and as in the other story types discussed, they take some element of the Negro stereotype and make it into a power device showing the Negro to be superior. Sexual superiority, the most common trait assumed by Negro men in these stories, is often found in combination with toughness and "style" (Abrahams, 1964, pp. 65–88). And in these jokes, sexual superiority is used as an aggressive weapon; most of these jests of the three men turn on the sexual proficiency and superiority of the Negro male illustrated either in the larger size of his genitalia or in his greater sexual capacity.

Three men were sent to court: a white, a Negro and a Mexican. They got to court and the judge said, "If you have fifteen inches of length between you, I'll let you go." The judge called for the bailiff to measure the penises. So he measured the Negro's and it was seven and one-half inches long. Then he measured the Mexican's and it was five and one-half inches long. Next he measured the white man's and it was two inches long. That was fifteen inches. Therefore they were set free. When they got outside the court, they all started laughing and bragging. The Negro said, "You'd better be glad mine was seven and a half inches." The Mexican said, "You'd better be glad mine was five and a half inches." The white man looked at them and said, "Both of you better be glad that I was on hard." [20]

A man put up a sign outside his farm offering a reward of one-hundred dollars to anyone who could make his alligator reach a climax. Three men came to try. They were a white man, a Mexican, and a Negro. The white man went in and stayed for fifteen minutes. He came out all tired and ragged. The score sheet reported: "Man—one climax. Alligator—none." The Mexican went in. He stayed for on hour. He came out haggard and disheveled. The score sheet read: "Man—four climaxes. Alligator—none." The Negro went in. He stayed two hours, three hours, twelve hours, a day, a week, two weeks. He came out neat as a pin, cool, calm, and collected. The score sheet read: "Man—fifteen climaxes. Alligator—dead." [21]

Another story in this cycle takes a more unusual trait, that of the purported strong smell of the Negro and utilizes it to exhibit, in another fashion, the hero's great masculine power.

Once upon a time there was a white man, a Mexican, and a Negro. They were in a contest to see who was the mustiest [muskiest]. So they tied a goat in the back of the house and said, "Now we'll see who is the mustiest." The white man went around the back of the house and the goat just sniffed a little. The Mexican went around the house and the goat sniffed a little more. The Negro went around the house and when he came back the goat was dead. [22]

The important term here is "musty [musky]," used rather than "smell" or "odor," for musky has strong sexual connotations, especially in a joke about goats. This joke is therefore something of a sexual boast. The Negro is, in a sense, beating the goat at his own game while putting the white man and the Mexican to shame.*

---

* Ironically, there is a widespread belief among Negroes that whites smell like goats or dogs with wet hair.

NEGRO AND ANIMAL

These last two stories are especially interesting in regard to the Negro stereotype because the heroes of these tales are not only in competition with the white man and Mexican but also with animals. The relation of man and animal is, in itself, an extremely complex subject in Negro folktales, but especially so because of the supposed animality of Negroes. Therefore, when a representative Negro beats an animal in terms of smell and sexuality he is being, in white puritanical terms, more animal than the beasts themselves. But as we have seen, this is simply a way of hyperbolizing his powers through the technique of contrast. This point is made in an overt way in those versions of the story of Lion meeting man, quoted in Chapter 1, in which man is "the Man." Dorson has collected a similar story in which Alligator learns to respect the Negro for his "powers."

The Alligator, the Whale, and the Colored Man

The Whale had never saw Man. So Alligator was going to show him a Colored Man. He said that Colored Man was a bitch with his ass. So the first thing they saw a have-been, an old man fishing on the bank. They swimmed on down the lake, and next thing they saw was a little boy. Whale asks Alligator, "Is that Man?" "No, that's a gonner-be." They swim on down a little further, finally they saw Man. He was on the back end of a boat. Whale he swimmed on back ("Man's a mess, he kills things"), he left Alligator there.

Alligator began to tackle the Man and the boat. The gas tank had just busted on the boat, and the Man was fixing to smoke. He took out a match, scratched his ass, lit the cigarette, and threw the match into the water. It blew up the gas, and knocked the Whale clean out of the water. He goes back to meet Brother Alligator and tells him, "Man is a bitch. He fetch up in his pocket and got him a match, which you call lightning. And he rubbed it against his ass, and threw it in the water and set the world on fire" (Dorson, pp. 102–3).

Stories of this kind make it clearer why Negroes do not hesitate to place themselves in competition with animals—it makes their powers seem that much greater when they win battles. Then when the Negro competes both against the animal and the white man and Mexican, he is showing himself to be that much more virile.

NEGRO AND WHITE MAN

This kind of aggressive statement of superiority in competition with whites is giving way to a further and even more overtly aggressive joke type. White man and Negro (usually a city Negro with great style and audacity) meet, have a fight when the Negro steps out of line and the white man is warned against reprisal by some very quick and forceful action and an accompanying statement on the part of the Negro.

> There was this Negro from up North visiting down South with some relatives. So he was just driving down the highway and he noticed his gas gauge showing empty. So without hesitating, he pulled into the next station. When he pulled in he noticed that the white fellow didn't come out to service his car. So he pulled his long Cadillac car over to the nearest tank, and shouted, "Give me a tank of gas." So the white fellow came out and said, "Nigger, don't you know who you are hollering at?" and reached in his pocket, pulled out a dime, threw it up in the air, pulled out his pistol and shot it six times before it hit the ground. During this time the Negro was checking out the situation and when the white fellow finished his act, the Negro reached into his car, pulled out an orange he had in the car, threw it up in the air, pulled out a long "Texas jack" [knife] threw it up in the air, and before the orange reached the ground it was peeled and centered. The white fellow looking at this quick action with the knife was amazed. So he asked the Negro, "Do you want the oil, water, and tires checked?" [23]

> One time there was a white man's rooster and a colored man's rooster. White man he went to the store and brought him a damn strong man's rooster. Colored man went to the store and bought him one of them poor-ass damned roosters. Damn white man's rooster wanted to

get up on the fence every morning and wanted to fight. Get up on the fence and look at the little colored man's rooster and go "Cock-a-doo. Who wanna fight?" The colored man's rooster: "I do." (spoken loudly and high) The white man's rooster would then just beat the goddamned shit outa that son-a-bitch. He goddam hollered and cussed but never could do nothing with the white man's rooster. Now this went on for two days. Two days later he got tired of seeing that white man's rooster beat shit outa his, so he went down and got him something. He went down and got him some spurs—you know, like a fighting cock has—and put 'em on his little rooster. Well, that rooster jumped up on that fence and went "Cock-a-doo. Who wanna fight?" "Urrumh" went the little colored man's rooster and just tore into him like a cat into a rat and just tore him to pieces. And that white man was afraid to buy another rooster. [24]

These stories illustrate the depth of the problem of Negro-white relations in the continuing situation in which whites seem to ask for acquiescence and subservience on the part of Negroes. The narratives show that the violent direction of recent Negro reaction to this situation that refuses them a sense of cultural and individual self-respect has been anticipated in their in-group humorous inventions. They directly portray Negro-white confrontations and show means by which at least some blacks feel they may gain a psychological advantage.

GROUP IDENTITY

To see these stories as *only* a reaction to white subjugation would be a vast oversimplification; lack of ego identification, especially with lower class Negro men, arises from the combination of a lack of employment opportunities for the men and a matrifocal family system which encourages an active distrust between the sexes (Abrahams, 1964, pp. 19–40). This distrust, further, prevails between age groups and between the religiously inclined and those who reject religion with its focus on the preacher. Consequently, there is considerably less of the sense of group cohesion that one finds in most other minority enclaves of the same size, and a real lack of total community leadership. Because the Negro has identified himself so strongly with the image imposed by the whites, his rejection and conversion of the stereotype can only be seen as a first step toward achieving a sense of personal and cultural identity.

The present lack of group identity is seen fully in these stories. They are totally hostile in their tone. The image of Negroes portrayed in them, though presented in positive terms, is still basically the stereotype imposed by the whites. This lack of group identity is further observable in the almost complete absence of definition of the stereotypes of other peoples. Insofar as there is a stereotype of the Mexican, for instance, it is just that he is somewhere between the white man and the Negro in his capacities. And the white man is simply defined in terms of what he lacks and the Negro has.

This does not mean that Negroes do not think and express themselves in negative stereotypes of other peoples. Rather, as a subordinated group their vocabulary of stereotyping traits is severely limited. As noted in the first chapter, stereotypes, when developed and utilized by superordinate groups reflect the values of the group expressed in negative terms. But when the negative traits of the stereotype become converted into positive characteristics, it is hardly possible to reverse the argument. Though smell may become a positive characteristic, the argument that cleanliness is a negative trait simply is not available to the black storyteller. He must rather fasten upon the feature of smell which the white man will lack by not smelling "strong"—sexual ineffectiveness. He has no developed sense of values beyond those provided for him—and in negative—by the white man. In other words, the majority-group's stereotypes assign traits as if they were not behavioral patterns but "qualities conceived as if somehow inherent in the objects" (Williams, p. 40). Negroes, insofar as they stereotype at all, can only conceive of others in terms of traits which they, the blacks, have and which the other groups do not.*

---

* This paucity of stereotyping vocabulary emerges clearly in Williams' book. He shows that the Negro has a stereotype of the white, but it is limited to statements like "white man hates me" (Williams, p. 247). Burma seems to argue the opposite, that Negroes have as much stereotype humor as whites, but his examples focus on the absurdity of "Jim Crow" situations, that is, those places where white man shows his hatred. This is corroborated by Cothran; he shows that lower class Negroes have three widely held beliefs in regard to whites:

This limited vocabulary of stereotype is not true of all New World Negro groups, not even those with similar histories. In the British West Indies, for instance, there is a large corpus of stories which not only articulate this same struggle of Negro and white but do so with a more clearly defined conventional characterization of the "Buckra Man" planter. Furthermore, in these islands one of the major forms of humor is the same kind of trio-contest jokes, with the important difference that the three involved are men from different islands—for instance, the 'Badian (Barbadian), the Vincentian (from St. Vincent) and the Trinidadian. And the differences are expressed in terms of dialect and of stereotype traits—the 'Badian is crafty and sharp, the St. Lucian is lazy and dumb, the Trinidadian a thief, and so on. One, therefore, can't help relating these lacks in American Negro storytelling techniques to the void of group-sense and lack of depth of cultural identity felt by the community as well as to the degree of rejection by whites, a rejection so stigmatizing and persistent that it has limited all recognition of other white traits.

This difference has been pointed out often, most recently by David Lowenthal in his discussion of race and color in the West Indies.

> Perhaps the most significant difference [between West Indians and American Negroes] is what the names themselves imply. To most white Americans, a Negro is still a Negro first and a man afterwards; the West Indian is a man from the outset in the eyes of the community and, therefore, to himself. The word "Negro," explains a Guyanese poet, is "A label denoting a type of human being who was part of a black minority in a white majority." In America "Negro" means problem. It had no application to the people living in the Antilles, where they form a black majority. Within the West Indies most designations are geographical. A black or colored man from Jamaica or Martinique is simply a Jamaican or Martiniquian; it is the white man who must establish his special identity. In the United States the opposite is the case. "Southerner" is invariably taken to mean "White Southerner"; the southern Negro is simply a Negro from the South (Lowenthal, p. 609).

That they are easily fooled by the flattery of "Uncle Tom" types; that white people do not care to be among Negroes; and that in general, white people hate Negroes (Cothran, p. 250).

Lowenthal's point stresses an important feature of the American Negro's lack of identity, his sense of being without a place both geographical and social with which he may identify and be identified. Without this, he seems incapable of seeing himself in terms of a distinct minority or ethnic culture. Lacking this, he can't conceive of the distinctiveness of other groups as well. Consequently, he uses a joke form which in most groups is an "ethnic joke" but which in his jests is shorn of any *ethnic* contrasts. The Negro jokes do play upon distinctions, but they are social rather than ethnic ones.* Given their restricted and subordinate state, Negroes have tended to see life in terms of social polarities: themselves as the excluded "have-nots" and the establishment whites as the "haves." Between the poles, as these jokes illustrate, he has been aware of ambiguous groups, peoples not "white" but somewhat above Negroes in terms of social acceptance. In the big Eastern cities, these ambiguous groups are commonly Italians, Jews, or Chinese, while in the Southwest the intermediate peoples are Mexicans. But, as these jokes show, these other groups are ill-defined in regard to distinct cultural characteristics; they are only seen to be between the Negroes and whites both in terms of social acceptability and in ability to perform certain acts of an ambivalent nature.

In this inability to distinguish groups in terms of linguistic or cultural disparity, Negroes are different from other so-called minority groups, such as Jews and Mexicans. In Texas, the social and economic situation of the Mexican is not very different from that of the Negro. However, "the Mexican-American . . . is quite aware of ethnic stereotypes. In contrast to . . . the Negro use of stereotypes, the Mexican-American jokes involve clearly defined ethnic slurs: the Englishman is arrogant and overbearing, the American is a check-writing millionaire who doesn't mind the cost, the Jew tries to push down the entry price into heaven, while the Negro is the happy-go-lucky, crap-shooting comedian" (Paredes).

* I am deeply indebted in the following argument to my colleague and friend Américo Paredes. We were both participants in the symposium, "Folklore and the Social Sciences," sponsored by the Social Science Research Council and the Wenner-Gren Foundation, at which I read a paper which contained part of the present argument, and he served as a discussant. He has kindly permitted me to incorporate many of his suggestions in this revision.

PLACE

The major difference between the situation of the Negroes and Mexican-Americans is that the latter have remained in an area which they once dominated and with which they are still identified (and are able to identify themselves). Further, though they are relegated to persistent subordinate status throughout the Southwest, they see around them evidence of their own continuing cultural presence—such as in the use, by Anglos, of Mexican style houses, furniture, clothes, and in the overwhelming regional popularity of Mexican cuisine. (Until quite recently one seldom heard of whites going to eat "soul food" at a Negro restaurant, though the cuisine *is* regarded as distinctive.)

That this continuing feeling of cultural identity is bound to a sense of place was dramatically illustrated in recent events in New Mexico. While Negroes were rioting to demonstrate the degradations of their mode of existence, destroying the very places—the ghetto—with which they are identified, Reies Tijerina was organizing a guerrilla band and "recapturing" Kit Carson National Forest from the Gringo Forest Rangers, and proclaiming their sovereignty over the land under the provisions of the Treaty of Guadalupe-Hidalgo. This action arose out of a sense of mission and was accompanied by the appropriate manifestos of purpose. In contrast to the protest-rioting of the Negroes, the Mexican-Americans were *in revolt*. Both riots and revolutions are aggressive acts, directed at "the enemy" whites, but one chose to act in the spirit of rebuilding a world once lost, and to do so with a plan in mind, while the other, reacting to restrictive policing, struck out blindly, destroying and looting (U. S. Riot Commission Report, pp. 109–200).

This feeling of lack of place is not unnoticed by Negroes. In fact, it is a constant theme in the Black Nationalism and Black Power movements. It is also a theme in some jokes of the type commented upon above, such as the following:

> There were a Mexican, Frenchman, Chinaman, and Negro sitting under a shade tree shooting the bull one afternoon. So they got to boasting about their countries and the Mexican said "Hail to the green

grass of Mexico that has never been surpassed by any country." The Frenchman said, "Hail to the great flag of France that is a symbol of power." The Chinaman said, "Hail to the Great Wall of China that has never been scaled."

Next it was the Negro's turn to boast but he hesitated because he couldn't think of anything to boast about. So just about the time he was fixing to give up he saw a blackbird that was flying over at the time, so he said "Hail to the blackbird who flew over the Great Wall of China, shit on the green grass of Mexico, and wiped his ass on the great flag of France." [25]

JOKES

The Negro jokes reviewed here are examples of one of the ways in which Negro-white relations are handled by an aggressive and ironic approach to life. Jokes, by their very nature, deal in stereotypes which we commonly call by their more literary name, "conventional characters." A joke commonly turns on a witticism and is consequently focussed on character interrelationships (without much depth of characterization, since the roles are representative and conventional.) The jokes quoted above also show that these interrelationships often turn into confrontations, conflicts which are usually resolved by the witticism, which points to the triumph of the witty or the strong. But jokes are short and therefore any illustrative actions are limited.

As we have seen, toasts are the other kind of traditional narratives which arise on the same joking occasions; they are longer, describe a series of episodes, and focus on heroic actions rather than on exercises of wit, chronicling the deeds of some "big man" like Stackolee as he acts with style. Therefore, they present values in terms of actions more fully than the jokes.

These epic poems, because of their length and emphasis on action explicate ghetto Negro values more fully than the jokes. They are more aggressive in tone and diction, though the hostility is not so clearly focussed on the white world, except in toasts like "Shine on the Titanic." In these toasts one can find the clearest exposition of the patterns of approved actions.

Most of these poems glorify being "tough," aggressive, masculine, powerful, easy to aggravate and quick to fight, criminal, and amoral. Any kind of restraint is a challenge to these heroes. The most widely known of these individualists are "Stackolee" and "Shine" both of whom, it will be recalled, become involved in epic contests which allow them to exhibit their masculinity in a dramatic fashion. Stackolee, beside killing a number of people who offer him only the slightest insult, has a gun-battle with "Bully Lion" in a bar called "The Bucket of Blood." "Shine," the only one of the toast heroes who actively contends with whites, has a series of wildly funny conflicts with the captain of the *Titanic*, his wife and daughter, the shark or whale, and finally, the Devil. One of the lesser members of this pantheon is the outlaw, "The Great MacDaddy" whose activities and attitudes are capsulized examples of the deeds of this bad-man type of hero.

The Great MacDaddy

> I was standing on the corner, wasn't even shooting crap,
> When a policeman came by, picked me up on a lame rap.
> He took me to the jailhouse 'bout quarter past eight.
> That morning 'bout ten past nine
> Turkey came down the line.
> Later on, 'bout ten past ten
> I was facing the judge and twelve other men.
> He looked down on me, he said,
> "You're the last of the bad.
> Now Dillinger, Slick Willie Sutton, all them fellows is gone,
> Left you, the Great MacDaddy to carry on."
> He said, "Now we gonna send you up the way,
>   Gonna send you up the river,
> Fifteen to thirty, that's your retire."
> I said, "Fifteen to thirty, that ain't no time.
> I got a brother in Sing Sing doing ninety-nine."
> Just then my sister-in-law jumped up, she started to cry.
> I throwed her a dirty old rag to wipe her eye.
> My mother-in-law jumped, she started to shout.
> "Sit down, bitch, you don't even know what the trial's about."
> 'Pon her arm she had my six-button benny.
> Said, "Here you are MacDaddy, here's your coat."

I put my hand in my pocket and much to my surprise,
I put my hand on two forty-fives.
I throwed them on the judge and made my way to the door.
As I was leaving, I tipped my hat to the pictures once more.
Now outside the courtroom was Charcoal Brown.
He was one of the baddest motherfuckers on this side of town.
The juries left out, and the broads gave a scream,
I was cooling 'bout hundred-fifteen miles an hour in my own limousine.
Rode here, rode there, to a little town called Sin.
That's when the police moved in.
We was fighting like hell till everything went black.
One of those sneaky cops come up and shot me in the back.*
I've got a tombstone disposition, graveyard mind.
I know I'm a bad motherfucker, that's why I don't mind dying. [26]

LIFE STYLE

It is this "tombstone disposition" which seems most characteristic of these badmen, because it illustrates a willingness to place one's life on the line, perhaps to die if only the dying can be done in proper style. And "style" in this case means not only heroic masculinity but with conspicuous consumption. Life is seen in commodity terms, with about as much worth as the personal limousine or the beautiful "threads" (clothes) which these heroes are often described as wearing. These outlaw heroes are regarded as heroic not just because they act aggressively in the face of authority, but they also announce that they are pursuers of the American Dream, with its visions of perpetual plenty available to those who are willing to do the pursuing. These are the Negro entrepreneurs, those who are going to grab the goods even if society at large seeks to keep the TV sets and the beautiful clothes in the windows of the department stores. These are those willing to be "a flying piece of furniture" for the privilege of flying around Main Street Heaven for at least a few hours.

The Negro, then, has been given an opportunity for making a choice, and he has taken it. But his patterns of emulation are still

* The anti-police motivation expressed here is also a common rationale for the riots. Both fictions and actions reflect a real antagonism, of course.

determined in great part by his conversion of the white stereotype. Further, his actions are still only arrived at through chance and made primarily in reaction to past indignities.

Through all this, there is a suicidal note in the activities of these heroes, as there is an element of the self-destructive in the riots. The tone of MacDaddy saying, "I know I'm a bad motherfucker, that's why I don't mind dying" is a clear expression of the ambivalence inherent in the Negro's situation. He accepts the immoral traits of the stereotype, turning them into positive attributes. Even badness is glorified if it enables one to partake more fully of the popular vision of the American experience. Crime, it is recognized, must be answered with punishment, even death. But death is one answer to the unmanageable conflicts of ghetto life, so badness may solve many problems.

The correlations between the conduct of the riots and the pattern of heroic actions are too insistent to ignore. In both jokes and life, ghettoized Negroes act in an aggressive manner which results in much violence and self-destruction and with a minimum of lasting rewards. But his frame of reference keeps him ready to act aggressively at any opportunity and to enjoy it fully when the chance comes. He holds his hostilities in readiness. Though he doesn't make programs for retaliation, and he doesn't have a clear sense of what he is fighting for, this is because he has little sense of identity except as described in white man's terms. Though he may feel he is striking at the white world, he rather turns any possibility of retaliation into an orgy of semi-directed destruction. He hopes the white world will look on these riots and see what will happen if things were directed away from the ghettos toward the great white suburban world. But the message of hope and potential violence seems bound to be misread, since it so firmly conforms to the conventional role-casting of Negroes as irrational thieving creatures.

But this does not mean that the rhetoric of the riots has been lost. Certain Negro militants have seen the self-defeating nature of the pattern but have recognized that the riots are at least a display of power that is noticed by the white world. They channel the aggressions outward, at least verbally. And they borrow the explosive, ambivalent rhetoric of the badman in framing their assault. Here, for instance, is a statement by Julius Lester, a young Negro folk-singer:

> I don't sing much now, because nothing short of destroying this country will satisfy me. . . . I love so intensely the beauty of humanity that I hate everything that frustrates, stifles, and destroys that beauty, and I will kill to see that it comes into being. To kill is often an act of love. And I learned that from a beautiful, shy young girl who is a guerrilla in South Viet Nam. She's killed 25 G.I.'s and I knew she knew about a love that I haven't experienced yet, but I look forward to experiencing it. I look forward to the day when I will place a person in my rifle sight, squeeze the trigger, hear the explosion and watch that person fall (Lester).

The focus here is a bit more explicit, the diction a little more extreme, but the tone and the "I don't mind dying" approach is the same as in the badman toasts and jokes. The question that remains is whether this is a verbal rationale for a deviant stance, or whether it portends future dramatically destructive Negro activities. We can be sure that given the chance, ghettoized Negroes are going to continue to take every opportunity that arises to act competitively, aggressively while seeking a sense of power, place, and self-determination.

4

People ravin' about hard times—
Tell me what it's all about?
Hard times don't worry me,
I was broke when they started out.

Love is like a faucet,
You can turn it off or on;
But when you think you've got it,
It's done turned off and gone.

I heard my baby call me;
I said, "What you want this time?"
She said, "If you ain't got a quarter,
Can't you give me a lousy dime?

I got so many womens
I cannot call they name.
Some of them is cross-eyed
But they see me just the same.

Let me be your sidetrack,
Baby, till the main line comes.
I can do more switching
Then the mainline ever done.*

To this point the discussion has centered on those items of black expressive culture which have openly or covertly confronted the problems of discrimination, white hatred, and social and economic subjugation. But there are many other persistent problems faced by blacks in their day-to-day lives which are the emotional by-products of subordination, and these problems and their solutions are observable in Negro folklore as well.

* *Traditional blues verses.*

In Chapter 3 data was presented which indicated that there was a correspondence between certain modes of approved action observable in jokes and toasts and activities. In a very real fashion, these traditional narratives which focussed on whites as the enemy presage overt anti-white violence—but they do not predetermine the activity. What both share beyond doubt was the presentation of the black involved in terms which conform to the white stereotype of Negroes and the black's stereotype of themselves as they developed this out of the white set of characteristics.

A misleading by-product of this argument is the implication that blacks are united not only in their reaction to white coercion but also in their attitudes toward the means by which they can strike back. Nothing could be further from the truth; if this were the case we would see much stronger evidence that blacks are involved in a revitalistic movement. It seems clear that both the riots and the anti-white folklore are methods developed to handle the constant expressions of exclusion provided by whites and at the same time to build black morale.

SOCIAL TYPES

While it was argued that due to subordination, the blacks had not developed an elaborate stereotyped image of "Whitey," this does not mean that Negroes have not developed a set of social types which they perceive within their own communities which are described in terms of stereotype traits. Men have stereotypes of women, women of men; the street-man has a fixed image of the Preacher, the Politician, the Storekeeper; street-corner society has a typology of its own denizens, pointing not only to "hard-men" or "gorillas," to "signifiers" or quick-talkers, to pimps, bulldaggers (lesbians), all manner of male homosexuals, to hustlers and to squares, to "nice" girls, "old ladies" (women lived with), wives, whores, to country-boys and city sharpers, and many more. These social types give insight into the variety of attitudes and life styles that exist within the black community, that illustrate the varieties of ways which have been developed to handle the problems of the economically and emotionally restricted life. These types populate black in-group fictions.

To say this is not to argue that these stories give a full or "true" picture of Negro life. Only some facets of life are fastened upon by the popular imagination for discussion in these fictions. But stories give voice to real and felt antagonisms; where they may depart from a realistic approach is in the manner of resolving the problems, for this may lead us into the realm of dream-life, of wish-fulfillment. (This warning is of greater moment in black-white fictional confrontations than in black-black engagements.) Furthermore, the stories do not represent the total range of Negro attitudes since they are primarily told by young men (and perhaps young women, though the evidence is not as clear) and therefore probably represent only one line of argument. Given these limitations, it seems worthwhile to survey these other stories for what they can tell us of the attitudes and preoccupations of black young men.

The "Cat" vs. the "Gorilla"

Though Negroes still seek the promise of the American Dream, the Eden he seeks is no garden paradise but a City of Gold and his values are those of urbanites not of peasants or would-be country people in spite of his continued reliance on the foods of his country past. The street-man exhibits all of the characteristics which used to be termed "dandy" with its emphasis on beautiful clothes and stylized manners calculated to attract attention. Furthermore, the Protestant ethic offers very little attraction. There are no frontiers in his world view, no new worlds to create for himself; paradise already exists but on the other side of the dividing line.

In this stylish world a job is convenient to supply money, but it is not something of which one is proud, especially since the jobs seldom are prestigious nor do they allow much hope for social and economic advancement. This is occasionally misunderstood by investigating social scientists. For instance, recently Charlotte Darrow and Paul Lowinger presented a paper on values of the rioters in Detroit and noted that: "Some young Negro males prefer to give the impression to their friends and peers that they are not working when in fact they are . . . He says: I don't have a job. I don't work at something that is degrading and humiliating. But still, I have good clothes and a good car." Darrow and Lowinger account for this by noting "that *because* having a good job is so important that an opposite effect takes over and there is a bravado about not working." They assume that having a job *is* desirable when it is not the job but the appearance of living the affluent and well-providing life which is often most important. And affluence is that much more dramatic if it exists without working for it, but rather by taking it (as with bad-men) or by having it given them (and not in the manner or the quantity provided by systems of relief.) The prestigious way of having style provided is by being able to manipulate others, to exploit them; and it would appear that there are two major techniques for exploitation—through an exercise of strength and endurance, or through a use of wits. As we have witnessed, the bad-man works through strength and attacking a problem directly. His opposite number is the "cat" who operates rather in terms of verbal persuasions whenever possible. Where the hard-man works through violence and direction, the cat exercises wit and indirection. The cat's *modus operandi* has been described by the sociologist Harold Firestone:

> He strictly eschewed the use of force and violence as a technique for achieving his ends or for settling of problematic situations. He achieved his goals by indirection, relying, rather, on persuasion and on a repertoire of manipulative techniques. . . .
> He used his wits and his conversational ability. To be able to confront such contingencies with adequacy and without resort to violence was to be "cool." His idea was to get what he wanted through persuasion and ingratiation; to use the other fellow by deliberately outwitting him. Indeed, he regarded himself as immeasurably superior to the "gorilla," [i.e. the cat's name for a hard-man] a person who resorted to force. . . .
> The cat seeks through a harmonious combination of charm, ingratiating speech, dress, music, the proper dedication to his "kick," and unrestrained generosity to make his day-to-day life itself a gracious work of art* (pp. 282, 285).

* By noting the artful dimension of the cat's existence, Firestone points to a further way in which life is seen in performance terms and values described therefore in terms of beautiful and ugly.

The "cool cat" figures in many of the stories in the Negro story-teller's repertoire. One series of jokes which have already been noted, has a formula opening such as "There was this cat from up North visiting his people down South, driving down there in Alabama in his brand new Cadillac and wearing his mohair coat and shoes shined like a mirror . . ." These stories commonly turn on some way in which the "slick" manages to trick the white storekeeper "Mr. Charlie" into giving him respect and service. Further, the cat emerges in certain notable toasts.

In these toasts, as in real life, the cat and "the gorilla" often find themselves in contest with each other to see who can carry off life in the better style. This very conflict is fully presented in the most popular of all toasts, "The Signifying Monkey and the Lion." The monkey is a well-known cool cat who gains his ends through indirection (this is exactly what "signifying" means). He uses "hidden language" extensively, bringing it to a high art.

> It was deep down in the jungles where the big coconuts grow,
> There lived the most signified monkey the world ever know.
> There hadn't been anything in these jungles for quite a little bit,
> So this monkey thought he would start some shit.
> So he hollered out to the lion one bright sunny day,
> Say, "Mr. Lion, there is a big burley motherfucker right down the way."
> Say, "Now I know you and him will never make friends,
> Because everytime you meet him your knees will bend."
> Say, "He got your whole family in the dozens and your sister on the
>   shelf
> And the way he talks about your mama I wouldn't do myself.
> And one thing he said about your mama I said I wasn't going to tell:
> He said your mama got a pussy deep as a well,"
> This lion was a mad son of a bitch;
> He jumped up and made a big roar.
> His tail was lashing like a forty-four.
> He left these jungles in a hell of a rage,
> Like a young cocksucker full of his gays.
> He left in a hell of a breeze;
> He was shaking coconuts from the trees.
> The small animals got scared and fell to their knees.
> He found the elephant asleep under a big oak tree,

Say, "You're the motherfucker talking about me."
But the elephant looked at him out of the corner of his eyes,
Say, "Go on, motherfucker, and pick on somebody your own size."
The elephant said, "My mother is very low sick and my brother lost
his life;
I got up this morning and found another motherfucker fucking my wife."
Say, "I'm telling you now in front of your face so you can see
This is no time to be fucking with me."
But the lion got back and make a forward
But the elephant knocked him on his hairy ass.
But he got back again and made a pass and the elephant ducked
And from this time on the lion was fucked.
They fought all night long and all the next day,
And I still don't see how that damn lion got away,
Because he broke both of his jaws and fucked up his face;
The elephant gave a yank on his tail and snatched his asshole clean
out of place.
Then back-tracked him through the woods more dead than alive.
That's when the little monkey came on with his signifying jive.
Said, "Ha, ha, motherfucker, look like you caught plenty of hell.
That elephant whipped your ass to fare-thee-well."
Said, "You left these jungles all highly sprung,
Now here you come back damn near hung—
With your face all fucked up like a cat's ass when he got the seven-
year itch
And you say you're 'King of the Jungle,' say now ain't you a bitch.
And every morning I try to fuck a wee bit,"
Say, "Here you come with that Lion roaring shit."
Say, "You're always around here roaring you're the king
And I don't believe you can whip a goddamn thing.
So shut up, motherfucker, don't you dare roar
Or I'll swing from these limbs and kick your ass some more.
And hurry up and get out from under my tree
Before I take a notion to shit or pee."
Now the little monkey got frantic and started to clown
When both feet slipped and his black ass hit the ground.
Like a flash of lightning and a bolt of white heat
The lion was on him with all four feet.
Then the little monkey with tears in his eyes
Said, "Oh, Mr. Lion, I apologize."

The Lion said, "Shut up, motherfucker, no use of your crying.
I'm going to cut out some of this signifying."
So the little monkey knew what was coming and he had to think fast
Before this lion tore a hole in his ass.
So he said, "Mr. Lion, if you let me off here like a good gentleman
   should,"
Say, "I'll whip your ass all over these woods."
So the lion jumped back and stepped back for the monkey to fight.
And about this time this little monkey jumped damn near out of sight.
Damn near the top of a long tall pine swing down on a limb
Where he knew the lion could not get him.
Again he came on with his bullshit and signifying.
Say "Now you kiss my two black balls and my black behind."
Say, "Yes, your mama got a cock big as a whale is true,
And your sister got a big cock, too!
And I started to stick a dick in your wife and the big cock flew.
And that ain't all—if you don't get out from under my tree I'll swing
   from one of these limbs and stick a dick in you."
Last time I was in the jungle, I passed the long tall tree,
The monkey was still at the top as happy as he could be.
But you can bet your life even from that day
The lion still wonders how that jive mother got away.
Now if anybody asked you who composed this toast,
Just tell him Bullshitting Bell from coast-to-coast. [27]

Here is a clear exposition of the different approaches of the "cat" and the "gorilla" in the characters of the monkey and the lion (with the narrator associating himself with the monkey by calling himself "Bullshitting Bell.")

The cat and the monkey are descendants of tricksters like Br'er Rabbit and the Slave John, for they live through wits and operate aggressively through indirection. In a city guise they offer a pattern of aggression and a life style which continue to be attractive to members of ghetto communities. But there is a felt opposition between those who would follow the cat's lead and those who subscribe to the ways of the bad-man. In my study of one group of men in Philadelphia, the values of the gorilla predominated. For instance, in a version collected there the "Signifying Monkey" was killed and in the one story about Br'er Rabbit collected there (and quoted here on p. 53), the wily animal is converted to a tough man who violently breaks up a party to which he has not been invited. Though "flash" was valued in this neighborhood, toughness was important, perhaps because most of my informants were ex-gang members. On the other hand, Bruce Jackson has found that in the toasts he has collected among prison inmates, less than five per cent of his texts are devoted to bad-men and a very large percentage depict the activities of pimps and slicks (Jackson, p. 4).

It is difficult to interpret the disparity in the street and the prison traditions meaningfully. But it seems possible at least to say that the two patterns of style and action have served as alternatives to the man in the street seeking self-respect and a feeling that he is in control of his own life by acquiring symbols of power and position. But both life patterns have heretofore been directed inward, bottled up in the Negro ghetto. Stackolee kills and rapes other Negroes and the Signifying Monkey directs his wiles against a bully-member of his own "jungle" community.

Recently both life patterns have been directed at the outside world and it is difficult to decide which has caused greater reaction in the white community. The "cat," in the person of a Cassius Clay or an Adam Clayton Powell, has suddenly forced itself on the notice of whites and they have no cultural equipment with which to understand him. Both Powell and Clay have constantly pointed out this cultural disparity, but their insights fall on deaf ears. Consequently, Powell was placed in a cat's blissful isolation in the Bahamas, surrounded by the trappings of the good life, while Muhammed Ali had his "World" heavyweight title taken from him for the "insolence" of trying to live by a religious creed that proceeds from coercive and separatist assumptions. However, such aggressive roles are not available to most Negroes. But it has suddenly become possible to put on the mask of the bad-man or the strong-man pose of the Black Panther in the licentious atmosphere of the riots. In such a situation, accommodation is forgotten and so is indirect attack. The symbols of power and place in American society are there in the store windows and in the counters and they are grabbed.

The monkey is often referred to as a "pimp-monkey"; in ghetto-Negro parlance, "pimp" is a laudatory term.* The pimp is, in many ways, the epitome of the cat because he is able not only to get clothes and money through the use of his wits but he does so by ruthlessly exploiting women. One pimp's rationale for this approach is just like that of any exploiter, anyone who subscribes to the coercive ideal and equates money and style with power: "Everybody in both worlds (white or black), kiss your ass black and blue if you have flash and front." The same pimp, "Iceberg Slim," gives us his vision of heaven in which style puts him in the position of God. He dreamed that he saw himself:

> . . . gigantic and powerful like God Almighty. My clothes would glow. My underwear would be a rainbow-hued silk petting my skin.
>
> My suits were spun-gold shot through with precious stones. My shoes would be dazzling silver. The toes were as sharp as daggers. Beautiful whores with piteous eyes groveled at my feet.
>
> Through the dream mist I would see shaped huge stakes. The whores' painted faces would be wild in fear. They would wail and beg me not to murder them on those sharp steel stakes ("Iceberg Slim," p. 77).

Just as the bad-man solves a moral problem through an easy and unconsidered decision to exploit through physical and violent usage, so the cat must decide that style or "flash" is best served through clever docility, verbal persuasion, or through convenient brutality. This means that he must be prepared, when he knows another is vulnerable, to become violent even though this may temporarily "blow his cool," the style on which he most commonly relies; it also means that he must be ready to become submissive when he knows that he is in a vulnerable position. His great weapon is his versatility, a characteristic which the hard-man, the gorilla lacks completely. Clearly to the cat an act of submission is admirable if it achieves or maintains status.

We see the difference of approach in the various toasts which turn

---

* "Pimp" as an adjective commonly means "sharp" or "beautiful"; the "gorilla" equivalent term in common black parlance is "tough" which means both "good" and "good-looking."

on a sexual challenge from a woman. When the challenged man adopts the bad-man pose the result is an epic fornication contest in which the man may or may not win, but he always performs admirably.

I'm from the Middle West;
I came by New York just to take a rest.
I saw an ad in the paper the other day, said there's a big affair in
    Chicago.
That's where all the big men like to go,
So I grabbed the Twentieth Century Limited, and went to that big affair,
Where a pretty little maid was waiting there.
She said, "Excuse me mister for being so fresh,
But would you like to go to my address?"
I said, "Excuse me, miss, for being so slow,
But my money is kind of low."
She said, "Where I live there's a hundred doors
And a hundred whores
A thousand dollar bet upon the wall
That no one man could fuck them all."
Now you can tell by my vest,
That I come on in any contest.
So I hoist my wings and grabbed this dame,
And down we strolled through the shady lane.
We came upon a whore house and knocked upon the door;
The landlady answered like a forty-four.
She said, "Who is knocking and won't come in?"
I said, "Big Dick Willie, and I came to win."
I entered the house and there's hundred whores lined against the wall;
They knew I came to fuck them all.
I dropped my pants below my knees,
That's when the landlady came to see.
But when I took out dick by the foot,
That's when the whores took *their* look.
I fucked ninety-eight straight without a stop;
That's when my dick got red hot.
I jived the landlady out of an oyster stew,
And promised her faithfully I'd fuck the other two.
I ate this oyster stew,

Quite naturally I *had* to fuck the other two.
I reached up on the wall to grab this bet.
She said, "Hold it Jack, you ain't won yet!"
So I grabbed the landlady by the waist and upon the bed I threw her,
And between her maiden thighs I began to screw her.
I threw her this way, I threw her that way, and asked if it suit her?
She said, "You can ram it, and you can jam it, just as long as you can
        bear it,
'Cause I've got a Goodyear Rubber pussy, and I'm damn sure you can't
        tear it."
I said, "I'm going to make it, and I'm going to shake it,
Just as long as you can take it;
'Cause I've got a hickory stick dick, and I'm damn sure you can't
        break it." [28]

When a cat finds himself faced with a similar situation, his reactions and his aims differ considerably. Here the conflict usually turns on whether the man will perform an unnatural sex act in return for wealth, and commonly ends, after some rapping, with a submissive act that allows him to achieve the life style to which he aspires.

Now this was while walking down L.A. street;
I was broke as hell but my clothes were neat.
I was broke as hell but feeling fine,
Just put the last I had on a fifth of wine.
So while I was standing on the corner of Eighth and Grind
Leaning against a lamppost and a three-pointed sign.
Thinking how I could make me some money
When a little fine voice says "Hey honey."
And I look around where I could see
And no bull shit this was a fine red head looking at me
She say, "Hey little daddy, when'd you get back in town?"
You know I was gonna act like I was in the know
So I said "Baby I just got back a few days ago."
She said "Well, I thought you and me was gonna out havin' a good
        time
Painting the town red buying whiskey, gin and wine."
I looked at her I said "Girl, that sound all right,

But, shit, I lost all my money on them dice last night."
She said, "Well, since I invited you out on this little spree
You just fuck the time. Leave the rest to me."
So now we made a few joints [marijuana cigarettes] and headed for
  Beverly Hills
Where you can't smell nothing 'cept roses and daffodils.
She drove up front of her pad, said "Daddy this is home sweet home,"
Said "This is the castle, but inside's the throne."
And no bull shit she had one of them red high tight pads, really corny
  and groovy
Just like one of them big-shot pads you see in the movies.
She said "Come on in Bitty and play your favorite song."
Say "Hell, I'm change clothes but it ain't gonna take long"
And she came out in one them gowns all skin tight
And I jumped square and done kissed her and asked her politely could
  I spend the night.
She said "Hell you can spend the night and the rest of 'em too
That's providing if you know what to do."
I says, "Now you wait a minute whore I'm kinda green
You break this shit down and let me know what you mean."
She said "Ah hell, I can find a grinder any time, that can grind for a
  while
But now tonight I want my love done the Hollywood style."
Say, "You got to get down on that floor on both your knees
Nibble at this pountang like a rat nibbling at cheese
Said you got to keep on nibbling and don't you lighten up and now
  drop
Till I pull on both your ears and say 'Daddy, please stop.' "
And that made me so mad that I began to shout.
I say, "Whore, I don't know what the hell you're talking 'bout.
Now I like cheese but I ain't no damn rat.
I go for a little piece of cock but not like that."
Say, "You're sittin' up there looking good in your silk and lace
But you'll never get to sit your big ass in my face."
She said, "Well Bitty there ain't nothing else you can do.
If you ain't gonna eat any of this cock I guess we through"
So I got my hat and coat and started to go,
But do you know I didn't get any farther than that whore's front door
She say "Hey wait a minute, little daddy," Say "Wait just a minute.
You might wanna eat some of this if you know what was in it,

Hell there's breakfast in bed for you and a diamond ring,
Bank-roll in your pocket and everything."
I looked at her and said, "Girl, eatin' a little cock all I gotta do
Shit, I don't see no reason in the world I ain't gonna string along
with you." [29]

These last two toasts are, in spite of their differences in tactics, remarkably similar in dramatic structure and in the particulars of the conflict. They are both told from the point of view of a "man on the make" and looking to "make" not a woman but money. Both heroes are, by force of circumstance, wandering in a strange place and there they encounter a situation which calls for the use of their talents, through challenges which happen to be embodied in the form of women. But the women are not the prizes for winning the contests; they are really the blocking figures. The prize, in both cases, is wealth and its associated style and status, achieved by the men either through stamina (in the first case) or through adaptability (as in the second).

Country-boy and Preacher

The cat and the gorilla represent alternatives of approved patterns of action. They are, in other words, two types of heroes with different attitudes and methods of operation. Because their activities are approved, these characters call for emulation. There are other social types portrayed in black stories who act in socially disapproved ways; rather than calling for emulation, their actions provide patterns of avoidance. As in most traditions, the activities of these characters are portrayed as childish and therefore ridiculous. In many ways these characters and the jokes in which they appear are more interesting in sociological and psychological terms.

The discussion, for the most part, has been directed toward humorous inventions, performances contrived to elicit wondrous laughter. But there are two kinds of laughter, one arising from a feeling of power and wonder at the audacious deeds of heroes in contest with villains, the other directed derisively at fools. American

Negro folklore, as the traditions of much of the world, has figures of both types—heroes and clowns. And the most evident foolish figures of Negro lore are the same as those found elsewhere: the country-boy and the preacher. However, though these clown figures are international, they are also pertinent and meaningful social types in Negro groups, and therefore humor directed at such stories is of more immediate interest and significance. The question that arises when encountering country-boy and preacher jokes, for the present purposes is not how Negro humor shares in an international fund of jests or how Negroes came to share in this fund, but rather why these stories have remained a part of the Negro repertoire throughout black America when other stories of international currency such as the Br'er Rabbit type have been rejected.

The image of the country-dweller is in direct contrast to the Harlem Cat. Whereas the latter controls the social environment wherever he goes, because he has learned proper style, the former is still living in a constrained social environment. When he is older and therefore should know better, the country-dweller is seen primarily in "Uncle Tom" terms. But this figure seldom enters into black humorous inventions except as a dramatic intensifier for the deeds of the city boy who goes South.

The country-*boy* plays a different role. Not only is he from the country, and therefore uninitiated, but he also is just an adolescent protected from life because of being stuck down on the farm. Consequently, his having no sense of how things are supposed to be done gives him license to do things which he otherwise could never do. The country may be socially restrictive, but it is a place of sexual license. The adventures of the country boy, then, are part of the important literature of license, recited for the purpose of giving voice to otherwise forbidden motives; license is given because the country-dweller, like a child, cannot be held responsible for his actions. Furthermore, the laughter which is directed *at* him emphasizes that his activities are to be avoided. So these motives can be expressed, with the rationale that they are being exorcized. This is true of clown stories in any culture, but especially important in Negro lore because the forbidden motive aired is that of incest, most commonly centering on sexual activity of the country-boy with his grandmother.

There was a young boy there [in the country] one time and he ain't never had no intercourse with a woman. So his dick got hard and his daddy saw it. "Son, what is that you got?" "Damned if I know, Daddy, I got to do something for it." He said, "O.K., come on." And he got a great big turkey and gave it to him. He said, "Now you go to town and the first woman get rid of that." Said, "You take and give her this turkey." So he went on by his Grandmama's house. She say, "Hey, what you gonna do with that turkey?" "Daddy gave it to me and told me to go to town and get a woman do somethin' for me." Said, "Ain't no use in you carrying that big old turkey to town. You might as well come on in here and let me fix you up." So he went on in there with his dick on hard. Went on back home, and his Daddy said, "Hey, did you go to town?" He said, "Did you get rid of that thing?" He said, "Yeah." He said, "Wait a minute. I want you to tell me who it was. Who was the lucky woman?" He said, "It was Grandma." He said, "Goddamn your soul. You mean you fucked my mama?" He said, "You're damn right. You fucked mine, didn't you?" [30]

This story not only permits the incest motive to be aired, but it also emphasizes an important element of this impulse; not only does the boy commit a forbidden act with his grandmother but he emphasizes that he is doing it as an aggressive act against his father, in retaliation for what his father had done to his mother. Furthermore, it is not the boy but the grandmother who is the real transgressor—a characteristic common to many of these country boy stories. The incest-motive is more commonly channelled away from the boy's mother or grandmother to those female relations of his girlfriend.

Now this is about a little old country-boy. Yeah, this is about a little country-boy. Little country-boy lived waaay out in the woods. Man he lived so far back in the woods he had to pack a lunch to go to the mailbox. Now anyway, he was going with this little old country girl. Now she told him, "Now listen here, you come 'round here 'bout nine o'clock, I'll cut the lights out, put the window up, right after you whistle and you'll know that I'm all ready." He said, "All right." He said, "I be there." " All right."

So now her grandmother heard it. Grandmother, she was about sixty-eight, sixty-nine years old. She ain't had no joint since Grandpop died 'bout twenty-five years ago. Well, she thinking to herself, "I'ma get some of this young peter." So just about ten minutes of nine, she said, "Daughter, you run down to the store, get me some snuff." She said, "But Grandma, store's almost thirty-five miles from here. Can I use the buggy?" "No, the horse is sick, you walk." "Grandma, I won't be back till 'bout four o'clock in the morning." "You go 'head." "All right."

So the little daughter thought she'd cut through the woods and catch up with Johnny, but Johnny duck 'round the other way. Johnny came in, looked up at the window and whistled. Grandma threw up the window, took off all her clothes and throwed herself in bed. Johnny jumped in the window, throwed off his clothes and jumped dead on that old fashioned cock. And Johnny started to work and shirling; after awhile he said, "Damn." He come to life, looked down and saw [it] was Grandma. He said, "Grandma, it's you!" She said, "Yes, son. It's me." He said, "Grandma, it stinks." She said, "Well, son, I'ma tell you, it's like this; it was just so goddamn good. I'm too old to come, so I just went on and shit." [31]

The country, then, is conceived of as a place in which one follows natural inclinations rather than conforming to social restrictions in the area of the appetites. The country-boy is therefore a figure to identify with vicariously because of his ability to by-pass restrictions, but because he is uninformed and often stupid, he is not to be emulated. On the other hand, the other foolish figure, the preacher, by-passes these restrictions (and many others) but for this he is condemned.

While the country-boy is a figure of fun, the preacher is ridiculed. The stories about the preacher emphasize his hypocrisy, the distance between his words and his acts. He persists as a butt of humor, therefore, as he embodies a social ideal, honesty, in negative form. The stories about "Preach" operate as a mechanism of social control. The attribute which is underscored is that though the preacher sets himself above other black men in his performances, underneath it all he is "just another nigger." Like the cat, he is capable of attaining status through ingratiation, smooth-talk, and shape-shifting; and like the gorilla, he has voracious appetites. But unlike these figures he is unwilling to admit to his drives, to his humanity, to his blackness, and it is this hypocritical approach that makes him a figure of ridicule.

The preacher's hypocrisy is brought out in a number of ways related to his life as a sermonizer and moral leader of his congregation. One of the most common facets of his hypocrisy is his tendency to seduce the women in his congregation, something at which he often gets caught.

This preacher had a mad crush on his favorite deacon's wife. Whenever he could, he would send the deacon out of town so that he could get to his wife. One day he sent the deacon out of town on important business and immediately rushed over to the deacon's house to make it with his wife who likewise dug him. They didn't waste any time and were hurriedly in bed having a ball not expecting anyone to call. Within a few minutes the doorbell rang. The deacon's wife told the preacher to get into the closet while she went to the door. The preacher rushed into the closet and closed the door on his balls. It was the deacon; he had forgotten his keys. When the deacon went into the bedroom, he saw the preacher's balls on the outside of the closet door and asked his wife what they were. She told him they were bells. So the deacon wanted to hear them ring. He tapped on them lightly and got no sound. He hit them a little bit harder and still got no sound. Finally he hit them very hard. The preacher yelled "Ding Dong, motherfucker, ding dong." [32]

Another attribute often found in combination with his sexual inclinations is his immoderate hunger for chicken. These two traits are juxtaposed humorously in one widely-told story.

This preacher he just loved two things in life better than anything else, and that was his deacon's wife's cooking and his deacon's wife's cock. And the deacon's wife seemed to really love to feed him, both ways. Preacher was always coming over after the sermon on Sundays and just eating up the place and the deacon's wife was always finding some way of getting the deacon out of the house after lunch so she and Preach' could go have some.

So this one time, the Preacher came over after the sermon and the deacon's wife asked the Deac' to go get some milk down at the store. Well, the store was way far away, so the deacon just had to know that something was up. So he pretended to go off to the store, but he really just went down the road a little ways and then he snuck back. There was the preacher just eating away at the Sunday chicken. He got hold of a leg and just really chomped at it, and then he got the breast and ate that too. Went through the whole chicken, the deacon's wife just looking on and enjoying seeing the preacher going to it. Ate the whole chicken.

So then they went into the bedroom and first thing you know, that preacher he started kissing her cock. Well the deacon was looking in the window at all this and he just couldn't stand it any more. So he burst through the door and really surprised them. He said, "You know, Preach', I don't mind you fucking up my eating, but I don't want you eating up my fucking." He really got the preacher on that one. [33]

The reverend is as equally adept at getting money from his women parishioners as he is at getting food and sexual favors.

This here one's about the time that the rev was collecting money—church collections hadn't been going very good for a while, you see. So he was visiting all the people in his church, at their homes. And he goes to this old woman's house and he asks her for a contribution. He said, "Whatever you give unto God, you will be rewarded ten times over. Whatever you give unto God, you will be rewarded a hundred times over." Well this woman said, "I don't have any money, but you can have my cow if that will do. But remember I'm to be rewarded ten times over." "You will, sister, you will!"

Well this old girl, she's going out there every day looking for God to reward her ten times over. Every day she's out there talking to God wondering where her reward is. Finally one day, she's out there and the reverend passed by and she said to him, "Reverend, you remember when I gave you that cow and you said that God would reward me ten times over for it?" "Yes, sister, I remember." "Well, I ain't seen no reward." He said, "Well, sister, you haven't prayed hard enough for it. You must pray to God and he will reward you." So she got down on her hands and knees and she began to pray: "Oh, Lord; Oh, Lord. You promised that what I would give to you you'd reward me ten times over." Just then this here bird flies over head and really lets go, right splat on her head. She looks over at the rev and she said, "Oh, Lord, Reverend, I don't want this shit. I just want my cow back." [34]

The most recurrent and potent source of ridicule, however, is pointing up the preacher's lack of power in preaching. All sorts of revelations come to be made in the midst of sermons, either through a slip of the tongue, or worse, by having a child or a parrot expose him. Such unmaskings underline the dishonesty of the preacher or show his religious powers to be considerably less than he claims them to be.

Now this here's about the reverend and the deacon. Deacon said he had a bull. So the reverend's family was in 'vation. He had a whole lot of kids, reverend didn't have no money, buy nothing to eat, so he went and stole the deacon's bull. So he invited everybody 'round. He even invited deacon over. "Come over to my house Sunday, 'cause right after church we're gonna have all kinds of beef." So the deacon said, "O.K."

So he came over and sat down, and he, you know how they do in the country, kids eat first and then the grown-ups. So the reverend sit down, and he said, "This here sure some good food. Um, um, um." "You know one thing, Rev?" He said, "What's that, Brother Deacon?" He said, "You know somebody stole my bull." He said, "Um, ain't that something, people just going 'round taking other people's stuff." And all the time he's the one that stole the bull.

So the kids were outside playing, so the deacon said, "I guess I'll go and sit out there in the back for a while, see the kids play." So at that time the kids had made up this here new game. Had each other by the hand, going around the circle singing:

Oh, Poppa stole the deacon's bull.
All of us children got a belly full.

So the deacon said, "Sing that song again. I'ma give you a nickel apiece if you sing that song again for me." So by them being kids and all, a whole nickel—you know a nickel's a whole lot of money to a kid. "Sing it again." So they started singing:

Oh, poppa stole the deacon's bull.
All of us children got a belly full.

So he said, "Thank you kids. Now I want you all to come to church next Sunday, and I'ma give you all fifty cents apiece. I want you all to sing that same song in church. 'Cause that there song carries a message." So they said, "O.K."

So they ran and told their mother that they were going to sing in church. So their mother was glad to have the children sing in church. She didn't know what they were going to sing about. So the deacon, he was going around to everybody's house, telling them, "Reverend Jones' kids gonna be in church, and they gonna sing a song, and it carries a message. And I want all you all to come down hear this here. The Lord sent them children to send this message. I want you to come on down there and hear them." So he went on over to Sister Mary's house, told Sister Mary about it. Pretty soon, he had gone to all the people in the community and the people had spread the word.

So finally that Sunday came. Children come to church, and they was clean. Well, by the time they got there, the church was so packed that so many people had to sit in the back of the church. So he told them, "Now when you go up there, I want you to sing loud so I can hear what you're singing, too." So they said, "Yes, sir, daddy, we gonna sing loud."

So the preacher, you know how the preacher do before he bring on the gospel singers. He'd go to preaching, telling you this and that, so he building up the people to hear this song. He said, "Yeah, ladies and gentlemens, you don't know. Kids can bring a message. Yes sir, kids can sure bring a message." He said, "Now just listen to this here message that Reverend Jones' kids gonna bring you. Now sing that song, children." They got up there:

> Oh, poppa stole the deacon's bull.
> All us children got a belly full.

So the Reverend in the back couldn't hear them. So he said, "Sing up louder, here boy. Come on now, sing up louder so I can hear you." By that time the people down front are looking at him. So he wondered what they looking at him for. So they started singing:

> Oh, poppa stole the deacon's bull.
> All us children got a belly full.

He said, "Look boy, I want you to sing it louder now. You all sing that song so I can hear it." So they got to the top of their voices:

> Oh, poppa stole the deacon's bull.
> All us children got a belly full.

So the reverend look and said, "Oh yeah? Well, children

> When you told that you told your last,
> Now when I get home I'm gonna kick your ass." [35]

There was this lady that had two parrots, a good parrot and a bad parrot. She would take the good parrot to church with her and would leave the bad parrot at home. One Sunday she was in a hurry and took the bad parrot by mistake. During the sermon, the parrot was perched on a rafter up in the ceiling. The preacher was just preaching away. He was saying, "I see God. He is in the church with us. He is all around us." The parrot looked all around the church, trying to see God. Then he rose up and said, "You're a lie, preacher. I am higher than you and I don't see a damned thing." [36]

One Sunday, this preacher decided to clean his church out. So he stood up in front of the congregation and said, "This morning, brothers and sisters, I want to clean out this here church. I want to separate the saints from the sinners, the good people from the bad. You must confess your sins. Now I want all the motherfuckers on one side and all the son-of-a-bitches on the other." So he repeated this, and everybody in the church got up and lined up on one side or the other except one man. So the preacher repeated, "I want all the motherfuckers on one side, and all the son-of-a-bitches on the other." Still this man didn't move. Preacher said, "What's the matter with you?" The man said, "Yessir, but you didn't call me." The preacher asked, "Well, what are you?" The man said, "I'm a cocksucker [a performer of cunnilingus]." So the preacher said, "Well, you can come on up here with me." [37]

There was this preacher that loved to drink. He would even take a bottle to church with him to nip on during his sermon. He would say to the congregation:

Sing a song and say a prayer
While I go outside and get me some fresh air.

He would duck out and get a drink.

One day, one of the deacons got hip to what was going on and stole the preacher's bottle. So the preacher as usual said to the congregation:

Sing a song and say a prayer
While I go outside and get me some fresh air.

He ducked outside and grabbed for his bottle and found out that it was gone. So he rushed back into the church and yelled:

Stop them songs and stop them prayers
'Cause some son-of-a-bitch stole my fresh air. [38]

———————

This preacher would always say to the ushers when it got hot while
he was preaching:
Open the windows and doors, and open them wide
So the Lord can come inside.
So this procedure was the same every Sunday.
Open the windows and doors, and open them wide,
So them poor sinners can come inside.
Or something like that. So one Sunday after saying his little sermon, he
said as usual:
Open those doors and open them wide
Let the good Lord come inside.
Well these boys were outside fighting and one picked up a brick and
threw it at another, but it went through the church window, right up
and hit the preacher. The preacher yelled to the ushers,
Close those windows and them doors and close them quick
'Cause some son-of-a-bitch done throwed a brick. [39]

There are numerous other jokes on the same themes, some like
these exposing the preacher as he is performing in the pulpit, others
showing him to be a charlatan in promising miracles such as walking
on the water (which proves to have a board just under the surface).
Through it all, the preacher is revealed as a drinker, a blasphemer,
a thief, attributes which when acted upon forcefully by street-men
are often positive traits. The reverend is ridiculed not because he
shares these characteristics with others but because he commits acts
while denying them. Even worse, he gets caught in his duplicities.

To understand why these stories have remained such a vital part
of the repertoire of the jokester one must remember that the street-
corner man-of-words has a real rival for word power and status in
the preacher. The street-man, whether he subscribes to cat or hard-
man values, is classified as a sinner, and as such is focussed upon by
the preacher in his sermons. There is a natural assumption by the
street-man that this occurs only as a way of garnering power, es-

pecially over the women in the congregation, thus being able to exploit them in terms of food, sex, and money. Since this is accepted as a norm (if not an ideal) for interpersonal activity, it is not the exploitation to which the street-man objects, but rather the rivalry that has proved in the long run, to be out of balance. In contests for allegiances and exploitability, the preacher always seems to win, thus the attribution of hypocrisy and charlatanism. And what makes the defeat all the more bitter is that the preacher is attracted to the same kind of life style as the street-man, with the Cadillacs, the beautiful clothing, and the retreat in the Bahamas surrounded by beautiful women.

The stories about the preacher, the cat, the hard-man and the country boy, give a reasonable picture of the male social types discerned by American Negroes, especially the men, themselves. Though in fictional relations with white men the black hero most commonly takes the bad-man pose (as opposed to his former image of trickster), in his fictions dealing with life among other blacks he is capable of a much wider set of attitudes and attributes. Through fictions of this sort we are capable of seeing some of the differing approaches to life proposed by black men. But they all agree on one thing: that life is primarily constituted of power-struggles, and that the proper end of life is to seize the initiative and to attempt to coerce, knowing that if you don't someone is going to exploit you.

5

♥♥♥♥♥♥♥♥♥♥♥♥♥♥♥♥

The next woman I get,
She got to have a job;
I'm not trying to be no pimp,
I just don't intend to work too hard.
I want her to buy the grocerie',
She gotta pay the rent,
She gotta fill up my car 'vry day
And give an account f'r every dime she spen'
I made up my mind,
If this is the way life gotta be,
I'm gonna do the same thing,
The same thing they been doin' to me.

She gotta make me think she love' me
By stayin' in her place,
And sleep in another room
So she won't be sno'ing in my face;
And when I ask her for some money
To go out on the town,
I want you to hand it to me smilin'
And don't you act no clown,
I made up my mind baby,
If this is the way life gotta be,
Yes, I'm gonna do the same thing,
The same thing they been doin' to me.

Now when I ask for some money
To go out on the town,
I want you to hand it to me smilin'
And don't you be no clown.
Now that might sound cold to you baby,
Or you might think I'm unfair,
But I been hurt so many times
Till I, I really don't care.
But I made up my mind, baby
If this is the way life gotta be,
I'm gonna do the same thing,
The same thing they be doin' to me. [40]

MEN AND WOMEN

Exploitation

The cat and the gorilla seem to agree on at least one subject; that women exist to be exploited. But not only do men commonly have this attitude—they also expect it from the women in return. Indeed, the women expect it of themselves it would appear. The blues singer B. B. King explores this coercive approach to life in cat terms in his composition above, "I'm Gonna Do What They Do to Me."

Elliot Liebow, describing the attitudes of one group of blacks with whom he worked closely, says of this vision of life in exploitative terms:

> Men and women talk of themselves and others as cynical self-serving marauders ceaselessly exploiting one another as use objects or objects of income. Sometimes such motives are ascribed only to women: "Them girls . . . , they want *fi*nance, not *ro*mance." But more often, the men prefer to see themselves as the exploiters, the women as the exploited, as in assessing a woman's desirability in terms of her wealth or earning power or in equating being "nice" with having a job. At a party, Tally waits for Jessie to arrive and grins with anticipation, "She's not pretty . . . but she's got a beautiful job."
>
> Men not only present themselves as economic exploiters of women but expect other men to do the same. When other men's

behavior does not meet these expectations, they claim not to understand the behavior (Liebow, pp. 137–138, 142).

Affection

This attitude of the men is counteracted by another and more sentimental view, in which protection and affection are the desired object, a point of view less expressed in the humorous inventions of the men than in the love songs to which they listen and applaud. These songs, which have become predominant in the "soul" repertoire, call for one of the partners to rely on the protection and the abilities to comfort the other. Even when this protective attitude predominates, there are strong ambivalences at work because of the insecurities of the men; consequently in approaching women they feel a pull between the strategies of the big-man ("I can satisfy you, baby") and the suppliant ("Love me, Mama, poor lonesome boy, a long way from home").

In this last approach, the model for the love-match becomes an idealized mother-child relationship. One important strand of reference in these courting songs revolves around the idea of the woman as "pretty mama" and of sexual intercourse as being lulled, comforted, "rocked." *

> Rock me, mama, rock me with all your might,
> Rock me, mama, rock me with all your might,
> 'Cause this loving baby needs you to hold him tight.
>
> Rock, pretty mama, please don't ever stop,
> Rock, pretty mama, please don't ever stop,
> Rock me, mama, let me blow my top.

This idealized mother-child relationship is an ambivalent image in itself because of the emotionally overloaded situation of mothers and children (especially male children). The early shock of separation occurs in most families because of the frequency with which new

---

* So, too, in songs sung from the woman's point of view, the good man is called her "daddy."

children are born, and almost nothing in the life of men or women in the black lower-class does anything to allay this separation trauma. Indeed, this type of insecurity remains the norm for both lower-class black men and women throughout their transient lives. As we have seen, mothers are openly castigated by boys for sexual betrayals in practices such as "playing the dozens." On the other hand, a feeling endures, even after the apron strings are cut by such procedures, that a mother's love can never be equalled by any other woman's. This attitude is often summed up in conversations by:

> Best time I ever spent in my life was in the arms of another man's wife
> —my mother.

This results in the paradox that the female principle is widely celebrated, almost worshipped by the men (and this is understood by the women and used by them in a number of ways) while women themselves are not to be trusted.

Sexual Approaches

The veneration of the feminine emerges most fully in numerous small verses openly dedicated to women and especially their genitalia.

> Here's to pussy that makes a man a fool;
> Takes away his worry, wears away his tool.
> Man gets on a woman, he hasn't long to stay;
> His head is full of nonsense, his ass is full of play.
> He gets on like a lion and gets off like a lamb;
> When he buttons up his britches he ain't worth a damn. [41]

It is not unusual to see a man using this image as a persuasive device in establishing relations with a woman. Rather than referring to her individual charms, he will place her in the female category and ask her simply to do what comes naturally.

> Here's to it, the birds do it,
> The bees do it and die.

Dogs do it and get hung to it,
So why not you and I? [41]

Such depersonalization serves as something of a rationale for the often impersonal sexual approach and the consequent changing of sexual partners. The implicit argument for this seems to be that "though I'm not true to you, I'm letting you be a woman and thus I'm being true to the feminine principle and therefore to my mother, too." Mistreating other women can thus underline one's loyalty to mother, not so much as a real life figure as a representative of an ideal (In real life she has let you down and often rejected you because you are not just her child, but also a man and therefore not to be trusted.)

Such a rationale is not fully successful in justifying male behavior to the men themselves, just as the norm of coercion is not. There are residual guilt feelings concerning infidelity, both to mother and to other women, feelings which themselves must be rationalized. This is done commonly by picturing men as supersexual animals who cannot control themselves when they see another woman. One of the most common of these animal images is the dog. Going from woman to woman is called "dogging it" by some, and the common term for male sexuality is "the dog in me" (Liebow, pp. 120–21). Another common animal figure for men is the rooster because of his freedom to tread all of the hens in the yard. In fact the story, which occurs in conversations about man's animal nature as a humorous explanation, equates man and the cock of the yard:

> This old man and his old wife were sitting outside on the porch back there in their one-room country shack. They were slowly rocking and looking around and here comes the rooster mounting all those hens. The old lady says to the old man, "Now how come you can't be like that?" He says, "Old lady, why don't you look close? That old rooster ain't mounting the same hen each time; I could do the same way if I was in his position, but if he had to stick to the same one, like me, he'd be old and tired too." [42]

The rooster and dog and other such animals recur in Negro songs, as well, like in the comic piece "He Wouldn't Stop Doing It."

> Our neighbor's rooster kept chasing our hen,
> We told him never let him do it again;
> But he wouldn't stop doing it,
> No, he wouldn't stop doing it,
> Last night we had some chicken stew—
> He'll stop doing it now. [43]

But the most common image, sung about in a serious context, refers to the lover as a dog:

> You got my stove so nice and hot,
> Oh, you got my stove so nice and hot,
> Oh, you got my stove so nice and hot,
> Then you laying around here trying to steal the meat out of my pot.
> Oh, you dog, wouldn't nothing else do it but a low-down dirty dog.
>
> I'm putting these biscuits in my stove for you,
> (But I wish you was dead, and I'm trying to kill you every minute)
> I'm putting these biscuits in my stove for you,
> Lying 'round here slobb'ing at the mouth and begging me for my bread.
> Oh, you dog, you nasty old rough alley dog—oh, you nasty dog. [44]

As in the last song, food and sex are often related metaphorically, leading to a large number of food images in love songs. Often the genitalia during the sex act are described in terms of food images; for instance, Bessie Smith sang:

> He boiled my cabbage, and he made it awful hot;
> Then he put in the bacon, it overflowed the pot.

while Jelly Roll Morton boasted:

> Now there's a lot of women ever-ready,
> Man, nobody can do the things I can.
> That's why they call me "Mister Jelly"
> 'Cause I sure know how to roll;
> There ain't no better jelly
> That's what I been told. [45]

This equation of food and sex is a "natural" since both are concerned with hungers and their satisfaction. Indeed, "satisfaction" is a basic concern of Negro concerns. The blues emotion, for instance, is often described in terms of some vague sense of dissatisfaction:

> I walked down the street, I couldn't be satisfied,
> I walked down the street, I couldn't be satisfied;
> I had them yo-yo blues, just too mean to cry. [46]

Most often, however, satisfaction is directly concerned with sexual matters, especially in the classic blues sung by women. Bessie Smith's repertoire, for instance, was replete with songs on this theme, such as "Press My Button, Ring My Bell":

> My man thought he was raisin' sand,
> I said, "Give it to me, baby, you don't understand.
> Where'd you put that thing? Where'd you put that thing?
> Just press my button, give my bell a ring."
>
> There's my baby, all out of breath,
> Been working all night an' ain't got nothing yet.
> What's wrong with that thing, that ting-a-ling,
> I been pressing your button and your bell won't ring. [46A]

In these stories and songs concerned with man-woman relations, sexual interplay is not conceived solely in terms of the aggressive male and the passive female. Women are presented, or present themselves, as being just as desirous and demanding of satisfaction as men. Furthermore, in many cases, as in the Bessie Smith song, they are pictured as having greater sexual capacity than men. With women, this is also associated with the animal within, though the animals are different:

> This guy was retired and he always wanted a farm. So he bought a farm but he didn't know anything about running it. So he bought a sow and he wanted to breed her. So every morning he took her down in a wheelbarrow to the boar-hog to breed her. You see he didn't know

that it took some time to have pigs. So this one morning he got up and went down to see if he had any pigs and the sow was in the wheelbarrow waiting for him. [47]

Sexual availability and capacity are, to be sure, part of the allure of women as females, but this can become a two-headed sword in some cases.

One time a man had a mule, you know, a pretty mule way back there in the olden days with a saddle on him, you know. He had the mule trained, you know, ever' time you goose him in the side the mule would break wind, you know, phhht. A woman standing on the corner, she say, "Give me a ride to town." He said, "I don't mind giving you a ride to town, but I got a deal." She said, "What is it?" He said, "Ever' time my mule break wind we gotta stop and fuck." She says, "Okay, okay." So they went on down the road a little bit, and he hit the mule on the side, you know. And the mule say "Phhht!" "Whoa! Fuck time!" He stopped and him and her fucked, you know. God damn, really giving it good to the woman, you know. They went on up a little further, about a mile or two, he goosed the mule on the side and the mule hauled off and farted again. "Phooo!" "Whoa, fuck time!" And he gave that woman a good fucking that time. Got on the mule and started on back to town. So she saw what he did. She goosed the mule and the mule broke wind. She say, "Hey, your mule done broke wind." After a while they got in there by a puddle of water where it was cool and a lot of trees. Hauled off and goosed the mule in the side. Said, "Hey, mister, your mule done broke wind. Time for us to fuck again." He said, "I wouldn't give a goddamn if that mule shit, I'm going to town." [48]

This picture of women as sexual creatures is not simply one projected *into* expressive lore. To the contrary, the image of the sexually demanding woman arises from real situations which the men themselves see as taxing. Once, while I was living in South Philadelphia, a young neighbor and friend came dragging into my place about eight in the morning. He had brought his attractive new girlfriend by the night before, and so the next morning I made some banter about having a hard night of it. He replied in an only half-humorous tone, "Oh man, she wouldn't let me go. She kept waking me up this morning saying 'Bobby, you didn't thrill me yet.'" That this situation is not uncommon is documented by Liebow, who discusses the complicated ruses developed by men to fend off their women when they are sexually fatigued.

> This predicament [of the men coming home from an engagement with another woman and being unable or unwilling to meet the sexual demands of their wives or women they are living with] is freely admitted to in an almost boastful manner. On the streetcorner, it is a source of great merriment, with each man claiming to have a characteristic way of dealing with it. Sea Cat claims that he usually feigns sleep or illness; Clarence insists on staying up to watch the late show on T.V., waiting for his wife to give up and go to sleep; Richard manufactures an argument and sleeps anywhere but in bed with Shirley; others feign drunkenness, job exhaustion, or simply stay away from home until their wives are asleep or until morning when the household is up and beginning another day (Liebow, p. 124).

This vision of women in regard to their infinite sexual capacities seems to be shared by some Negro women themselves, for traditional stories collected from them seem to make the same point; here is one, for instance, which not only discusses the sexual capacity of women but does so in regard to a difference in cultural aptitudes as well. It comes from a female informant.

> There were three little girls in school. The little gray [white] girl's name was Angelia; the little Spanish girl's name was Maria; and the little Negro girl's name was Mary. The teacher said, "Angelia, honey, spell 'Peter.' " Angelia said, "P . . . , p-e . . . , teacher that's too long." Teacher said, "That's all right, baby." She went on to the Spanish girl. She said, "Maria, spell 'Peter' for me, honey." Maria said, "P . . . , P-e . . . , teacher, that's too hard." Teacher said, "That's all right, baby." She asked the little Negro girl, she said, "Mary, spell 'Peter' for me, honey." The Negro girl said, "P-e-t-e-r, they don't come too long and hard for me." [49]

The force of this joke is that a man's genitalia and performance ability place individual men in an equally impersonalized role—as they say, "just filling a hole in their lives."

The male view of women is, in other words, paralleled by the female view of men. Though both cling to sentimental ideals of what the other *should* be in relationships with each other and with their children, neither seems to expect the other to come close to this ideal. Men say repeatedly that no woman can be trusted, while in the same breath they may distinguish between usual girls and "nice" ones that are worthy of respect and love. The same distrust is voiced by women while they continue to look for a man on whom they can depend. Even more important, the cynical attitude is voiced by mothers to their children, whether male or female, and often in regard to the children's fathers, bringing about a very dim view of fatherhood and responsibility, but establishing the basis for the distinction for the real and the ideal (fathers let you down; mothers don't).

An image of intersexual relations is consequently presented which turns on the existence of uncontrollable sexual drives, which is sometimes, but not always, accompanied by a conventional sentimental attachment to the other person. This rationale permits sex to occur in the midst of a situation of active distrust on the part of both performers; both assume the other is both involved in some sort of exploitation and playing out a drive.

The image of the lower-class Negro life presented here is singularly focussed on self-interest. In an environment that is charged with immense insecurities, individuals soon learn that they have only themselves and their own abilities to fall back on. Yet, as anyone knows who has spent time in a Negro community, there is a great deal of social interplay there. The problems of maintaining social and sexual relationships are profound in such a milieu; the techniques of socialization are consequently complex. Understanding Negro concepts of friendship and love is central to an understanding of the nature and texture of their interpersonal relationships.

Interpersonal affect levels tend to remain very low in most liaisons; otherwise they tend to burn themselves out, for as soon as circumstances make one of the partners feel guilty through a feeling of obligation and an inability to live up to this reliance through a lack of requisite economic or psychological resources, the relationship becomes emotionally overloaded and some excuse is found or manufactured to break it up. Coercion and exploitation, as norms, function as much to ensure this low affect level in interpersonal relations as to give weapons for fighting the battles of life. Conflict as a norm is convenient for those who are constantly faced with the possibility of losing the battle for it gives a built-in rationale for—indeed, an expectation of—failure. In fact, the economic battle *is* doomed to failure for most lower-class blacks because of the difficulty of finding a job with any kind of security or advancement potential. This failure provides the model for the others in the more interpersonal realms of life.

Among other things, this severely affects attitude toward both time and money. No one can develop a sense of the future unless there is something presented of value to which he may look forward (Horton). There can be little looking forward to tomorrow, except to dream of some fantastic delivery from wanting and needing, for those who have learned that tomorrow will more often than not bring another set-back, another humiliation, another dramatic recognition of one's inabilities and failures. Under such circumstances, relationships of trust and mutual obligation are almost impossible, and this is as true of friendships as it is of love affairs.

FRIENDSHIP

Among the materials I collected in Philadelphia was a notebook of typed jokes and toasts that had been made up by one of the men in the neighborhood in which I was living, typed out at the place in which he worked. Many of the items in it were from the repertoire that was familiar, and one or two pieces were from the standard international tradition of pornography (like the "sleeve job" story). But there was one story I did not understand until recently, for it seemed more a poignant picture of life than a joke or recitation.

"Surprised"

It was December 23, 1953, when my husband rang the doorbell, which I didn't know it was him. I opened the door and there he stood.

He cried, "Doris, my darling," and pulled me off my feet, and smothered me with waiting kisses, saying that he loved me, and missed me so very much. I knew that he had to miss me because he was gone away from home 22 months and what he hadn't known that someone else had been taking out what he misses so much. Then all at once Bobby, Richy, and Joan came running up to him crying "Daddy, daddy, daddy!" He let me go and picked them up one at a time kissing and hugging them, and then that moment came. My new baby let out a noise from the crib in the bedroom. My husband said "Who was that?" I didn't know how to reply to him. He went into the room and seen my new baby and then Bobby told his daddy to pick up his little sister. John, my husband, said that "Joan was his sister." They said no, was Tillie, the one in the crib. Then I told him yes it was my baby, and picked her up. He asked me was it any of his friends? Then he started to name a half a dozen or more. He asked, "Was it Raymond?" I said, "No." "Joe?" I shook my head meaning no again. "Robert?" "No." "Bill?" "No." "Herbert?" I said no this time real loud, and meant it so that he wouldn't ask me any more, and told him that he wasn't the only motherfucker on earth. And then I told him that he wasn't the only one that has friends; they were some of *my* friends.

The effect of this self-conscious story relies upon not so much the deception, which is taken for granted by the participants while seemingly lamented by both of them, but on the importance of having "friends" of one's own. This provides the direction and force of the narrator's final rejoinder. To understand the nature of this quip it is necessary to realize that lovers and friends are often at cross-purposes in a world of the exploiting and the exploited. One of the solutions to the recurrent problems engendered by a lack of interpersonal trust is to develop a large and constantly changing network of personal contacts. One of the reasons a man likes to have on-going sexual liaisons with a number of women seems to be that this gives him a feeling that the larger number of people upon whom he can call for something (sexual, financial, or otherwise) the greater his base of operations and the more protected his self-esteem will be. Depth-relationships, made impossible by the uncontrolled circumstances, are made up for, in part, by relationships in breadth (Liebow, pp. 16–20).

This frame of reference results in an expectation of change, both in the nature and intensity of relationships and in the configuration of one's personal network. Life is therefore conceived of in terms of a series of encounters with a large number of individuals; though transactions with others may repeatedly exhibit the same interactive patterns, this is not often recognized because the faces are different. When one relationship proves to be a failure, there is an implicit understanding that there will be others.

This constant fluctuation of personal relationships is given some manner of stability through a number of verbal activities. Most important perhaps is the fact that one finds oneself in constant contact with others in the same situation, with whom one may therefore repeatedly rehearse the various approved rationales for not developing relationships in great depth (especially with the other sex). This often involves a choral demonstration in groups in which one or another is faced with an emotional crisis. The one most affected will make some statement of his troubles, such as having had a fight with his "old lady" and someone else will either recite a similar situation in which he has been involved, or he will make some statement about how all women are the same. This will call for a number of reiterations of the same type, often in proverbial form, such as "If all women (or men) was as to their country as they are to their men, goodbye country"; or "A woman has many faults but a man has only two: everything he say and everything he do." In this way, one part of one's network is able to help with the emotional-situational dimension of a problem brought on by another sector of the network. The troubled person solves his problem by depersonalizing himself, by allying himself with a category of individuals in which other members of his network fit; this produces a feeling of temporary community of interest without necessarily involving any further emotional commitment on the part of individuals in the consoling chorus.

Another somewhat impersonal means of providing stability to one's network is through the use of gossip. By this I do not mean malicious talk, but simply any kind of talk about others. In the midst of constant fluctuation of relationships, one can feel in touch with a large number of people as long as one hears about them and knows where they can be found. Consequently, whenever an old friend is encountered there follows a formulaic recitation on the part of both as to whom one has seen lately, what they are doing, where they are living, and so on. This is punctuated by indications that other similar conversations have been held recently, between mutual friends. To be sure, this kind of dialog is common to any friendship group, white or black. But it is more important in lower-class black groups, for it is through such conversational means the breadth of the network is maintained at its outer limits, and self-esteem is mutually enhanced without any necessity to demonstrate friendship at any emotional cost.

To one who is rooted in a set of associations which are fairly constant, as are most middle-class Americans, it is difficult to imagine the way in which personal networks fluctuate in lower-class black life. One of the strangest feelings for someone moving into a ghetto from a bourgeois background is the way in which friends will disappear for days, months, even years, without saying goodbye, and will drift back with a minimum of comment and explanation. One of the few counteracting forces to this disorientation is hearing about the friend from others who have bumped into him in another neighborhood or gotten a letter from him from jail. Questions about this fluidity in interpersonal involvements will most commonly be answered by others in that person's network with an incredulous giggle or a statement that indicates that this is the price of living life in terms of a series of crises: "his old lady threw him out"; "the police were after him"; "his wife took him to court and he had to lose himself or go to jail for nonsupport."

We have already noticed that there is an esthetic pattern in Negro narratives that corresponds to this vision of society as a constantly changing network of involvements; black heroes like Stackolee and Shine prove themselves through a series of encounters of others who have challenged them, while other figures like Toledo Slim have a similar string of run-ins, with a less successful outcome. There is a further esthetic dimension that parallels this reliance upon a wide network of acquaintances. A number of toasts are composed, in part, of a simple listing of people recognized by the poetic speaker in the setting of the drama. The idea in such passages seems to be that simply recognizing powerful figures allows one to share in the power. One notable composition catalogs a whole pantheon of outlaw heroes. This toast is concerned with the doings of Jesse James and his gang, but at one point the narrator gazes around and sees many others!

> . . . But don't get me wrong.
> The James Brothers weren't the only badmen on the train.
> There were the Dalton Brothers, four of a kind.
> They shot a motherfucker for a raggedy dime.
> There was John Dillinger in the corner, counting his gold.
> He shot his motherfucker when he was ten years old.
> There was a bad motherfucker in the corner we all should know.
> *His* name was Geronimo. [50]

Even more focussed on security in the friendship-network are those toasts that catalog a list of people by nicknames. In one, the narrator walks into a bar and describes those present with this flourish:

> Over in the corner sat Sweet Jaw Lucy, looking all juicy,
> With Half-Head and Stumblin' Joe Blue;
> With Joe-Joe the Rabbit, the bustling girl's habit,
> And Tough-Pen and Tough-Toothed Old Sue;
> They sat with Ninety-Proof Mary and Old Pure-Grained Jerry
> Sitting with Spic-Eating Mick:
> With Creepty McFarer, the storekeeper's terror;
> With Big Dick and Struggle-Face Jack;
> With Whippy-Top Ed, who was crazy in the head,
> And next to him, Tiger-Tooth Dan;
> Say there was a whore named Vi, looking all spry,
> With Quincy, the big numbers man.
> Old Rump-Tump Fanny and Mumble-Trump Annie,
> Stood talking to Bad-Eye Windine,
> When all eyes turned right as old Saw-Toes Spike
> Eased in sportin' a cashmere vine (suit),
> With the professional killer named Sticky Sam Miller
> Who covered him well from behind. . . . [51]

This emphasis on knowing a large number of people does not mean that fidelity in friendships is not valued. Indeed being "up tight" with someone, having him as an "ace boon coon," is a state which is much admired and much celebrated in casual talk. Elaborate vows of friendship, in terms of "going for brother and sister" or being "cutting buddies," are often testified to. But friendships, like love affairs, are most often brief because they must end when a conflict of interest arises and the two begin to see each other in terms of adversaries. "Extravagant pledges of aid and comfort between friends are, at one level, made and received in good faith. But at another level, fully aware of his friends' limited resources and the demands of their self-interest, each person is ultimately prepared to look to himself alone . . . [this] leads to the assessment of friendship as a 'fair weather phenomenon,'" (Liebow, pp. 180–81) a view not far from the truth, especially in crises.

The constant communication of the extent of one's network is necessary for its operation in the maintenance of self-esteem. Therefore, not only do numerous names of friends come up in conversation, but there is also discussion of how friends should act with each other and how relationships can be maintained or destroyed. American Negro enclaves share with Afro-American communities throughout the New World a predilection for expressing ethical subjects in proverbial form. Consequently, discussions of personal relationships are punctuated not only by professions of liking and disapproval but also by abstracted comments on the criteria for proper behavior. For instance, on the subject of friendship it is widely felt that *too* much talk of another will turn malicious and threaten the superstructure of esteem, a problem commented upon by the proverb "That's why a dog has so many friends—he wags his tail and keeps his mouth shut," and "A fish would never get caught if he kept his mouth shut." Truth between friends is often spoken of as ideal in a relationship (though not really expected), a point made admonitorily in such sayings as "He who lies will steal" and "signifying is worse than dying." It is not unusual to hear third person reports of "bad-mouthing" or "down-talking" answered by very artificial statements as "He who steals my purse steals trash, but he who steals my good name steals great riches." And to someone who professes friendship but who will not share with friends when he gets some money, there are a number of strong proverbial statements like "No matter how high is a feather, he's gonna come down."

"Up" and "down" are a pair of words that constantly enter into conversations. Their use in the context of verbal and sexual contest has already been commented on. But, in a larger sense, being up or down refers to one's position not only in relation to other people but to impersonal fortune. "Getting up" and "being up" are desirable conditions because of increased self-esteem, in terms of personal power in contest and in terms of having a great many friends.

The weak point in such a way of looking at life is that this merely underscores the "fair weather" dimension of friendship. Consequently, most of the traditional expressions on the subject of friendship come from the view from below, from the down position, and are both admonitions and complaints. "Friendship," it is argued, "is a sometime thing"; "When you're up, funny thing but the whole world's up with you; but when you're down, you're down there all alone." And being all alone is, in this system of building self-esteem on breadth of friendships, a shattering experience. This is the point of the song, made famous by Bessie Smith (and more recently, Josh White), "Nobody Knows You When You're Down and Out" written by Jimmy Cox.

> Once I lived the life of a millionaire,
> Spending my money, I didn't care.
> I took all my friends out for a good time,
> Buyin' high price liquor, champagne and wine.
> When I began to fall so low,
> I didn't have a friend and no place to go;
> If I ever get my hands on a dollar again,
> I'm gonna hold on to it till the eagle grins.
> Nobody knows you when you're down and out.
> In your pocket not one penny,
> And your friends, you haven't any.
> But if you ever get on your feet again,
> Then you'll meet your long lost friends.
> It's mighty strange without a doubt,
> Nobody knows you when you're down and out. [52]

The same message—that friendship exists where exploitation possibilities exist—is conveyed in a toast on the subject in which the relationship between proverty and lack of friends is not only stated but dramatized.

I used to be rich, and then I was right,
Spending all that money just like I was white.
Then one day I found I was broke, and not a friend did I have,
Those whores they looked past me like I was coming from the grave.
So I went to this friend I used to show a good time
And I walked down the street and asked him for a lousy dime.
He said, "You're a friend, I know that it's true,
But if you want a dime from me here's what you got to do:
You've got to walk the waters like Jesus trod the seas;
You've got to get some thunder and lightning and bring it on back to me.
You've got to swim two, three oceans around and 'round;
And when you swim the Pacific you've got to tell me you ain't drowned.
You've got to put half a hundred and twenty-fifth street in a sack,
Then throw that motherfucker around your back.
Now if you do this in one hour's time
Then I'll introduce you up to a friend of mine
Who *might* lend you a nickel, but not a dime." [53]

Such pieces emphasize not only that friendships are frail but that the test of a friendship is always in terms of exploitability. We noted in Chapter Two that a large number of Br'er Rabbit stories dwelt on the theme of the dissolution of friendship, and served as cautionary tales. These stories are now seldom much of a part of the repertoire of the street-corner entertainers, but they have been replaced by animal parables in which friendship is demonstrated by one animal teaching another how to exploit the "things" in his environment properly.

You know these two bulls were standing upon the field, you know way up on the hill. Down in the valley was a whole lot of cows. Now the young bull looked at the old bull—you know this old bull he had been in the bullfighting ring in his day and he was a very old bull—so the young bull he was spry, jumping around and healthy, all full of pep. He said, "Look here, old bull, let's run down in the valley and fuck a few of those cows." Old Bull looked at him and said, "Son, if you take your time, we *walk* down, we might fuck 'em all." [54]

You know this young dog was standing there talking to the old dog. He said, "Young dog, you ain't been out in the world yet, is you?" Dog said, "No, sir." He said, "I'ma show you what life there is out here." He said, "All right." "Everything I do, you just come along behind me and do the same thing." "Yes, sir." So the dogs they walked out and walked down the street, and old dog got to a pole, smelt the pole, cocked the leg, and he peed on it. So young dog cocked *his* leg and peed. So they walked along and old dog came to a car. He walked around the car, he looked at it, smelt the car, cocked his leg up, and he peed on that. So the young dog, he walked up, smelt the car, cocked his leg up, and he peed on it. The old dog he walked down to the garbage can, looked over the side, got himself a bone and ate it. The young dog, he walked over to the garbage can, looked over the side, got *him*self a bone. So they walked on for maybe ten or fifteen minutes, they saw a she-dog. Old dog smelt her, kissed her, walked around, jumped up on her, knocked himself off a piece. So the young dog he walked up to her, kissed her and he smelt her, jumped up on her, knocked *him*self a piece out. So they went back on down, you know, to the yard. Old dog said, "Well, son, how you like the world?" He said, "It's complicated." "What you mean?" He said, "Well, now, er uh, we went down, walked, came to a pole, smelt the pole, then we peed on it. Came to a car, we looked it over, smelt the car, and peed on that. Then we walked down, seen a girl, kissed her, and even smelled her. Then we did it to her. That was all right. Even when we went to the garbage can, got something to eat. I guess it was all right. But what's the basis of being out in the world? I don't see no future in it." He said, "Well, son, take the advice of an old dog. Anything in this world that you can't smell, eat, kiss, or fuck, piss on it." [55]

The effect of the lower-class blacks' coercive attitude toward interpersonal relationships is only slightly modified by the ideal of friendship. In some respects, friendship and a stable man-woman household arrangement are perceived to be antithetical, for it is one's friends who take one away from the home and who "bad-mouth" one's partner. In such situations a number of traditional arguments are given by friends: "she'll just go off with another man," "she's getting down on you to her friends," "you can't trust any of them," and so on. The real rationale behind these arguments is that friendships last longer than love-matches.

In the last ten years songs have shown an increasing concern with the theme of keeping love-partners together. One such composition, by Bobby "Blue" Bland is in modified traditional blues form and style and uses a straight economic argument.

> Don't let your friends turn you against me, babe,
> Because they ain't giving you one red cent.
> Woh, Oh, don't let your friends turn you against me, babe,
> Because they ain't giving you one red copper cent.
> I say, when I leave you this time, baby,
> I just want to know who' gonna pay your house rent?
>
> (I said one more time)
> Don't let 'em turn you against me, babe,
> And this time I'm gonn let your conscience be your guide.
> Woh, Oh, don't let 'em turn you against me, babe,
> This time I'm gonna let your conscience be your guide.
> Woh, Oh, and when I leave you this time, baby,
> I just want to know will your friends stand by your side?
>
> (chanted)
> Your friends say that I'm no good,
> I hunt women like a dog hunt a bone.
> But I can't be doin' too much wrong, baby;
> Every week I bring my paycheck home.
> So don't let 'em turn you against me, baby,
> And I know you're blind and you just can't see,
> I said, you better get hip to all girlfriends,
> They just trying to get next to me. [56]

B. B. King also sings a song on the same theme, but from the point of view of a relationship that has already been ruined by gossiping friends.

Oh, you let your friends turn you 'gainst me,
With the things they been tellin' you.
You let our friends turn you 'gainst me,
With the things they been tellin' you.
And now that I'm goin', woman,
Can you see what they are doin' to you?

Oh, some people don't want you happy,
But they won't come right out and say it.
Oh, lot a people don't want you happy, little girl,
But they won't come right out and say it.
Yes, they just lie a little now and then, baby,
Just to keep you thinking that way.

Oh, now that you've lost me, baby,
Do they pay your bills when due?
Oh, now that I'm gone,
Do they pay your bills when due?
Or do you have to get out, baby,
And do all those things I used to do for you? [57]

The other side of the argument is that loves come and go, but it is your friends who stay and provide you with the greatest amount of stability. Ultimately, however, there is a recognition that with both friends and lovers, as another of B. B. King's songs preaches, you have to "pay the cos' to be the boss."

But in the lower class black situation it is impossible, all too often, to "pay the cos'." Therefore, because they are unable to maintain the ideal love-friend-provider relationship of man to woman, individuals must cling to their proven and adaptive base of operations—the friendship network. Where income is irregular and insufficient, it is necessary to exploit friend and kin. Transience guarantees maximum security. Through this, all those in the network remain economically and socially equal, providing a community of individuals who will remain on about the same level. Even if one member is suddenly able to raise his situation (thus "getting up"), by hitting numbers for instance, chances are good that his friends will remind him of their presence and that his habit of thinking in network terms will cause him to share some of his money or to suddenly because transient. This accounts, in large measure, for the pervasive lack of hope or trust in the future, the continued low affect level of relationships, and yet a strong feeling that there is a community of interest in such groups.

6

☞ ☞ ☞ ☞ ☞

"A house is on fire, pretend. You're sleeping next to your partner. You open one eye and you see the house is on fire. Your partner's still sleeping. And you see this hot lava and this burning two-by-four is getting ready to fall on your partner, and you get out of the bed. You run out of the house without waking him up!

"When you get outside, you say, 'Oh, Lord, what have I done wrong? I was so selfish and greedy and worrying about myself until I forgot about my partner inside. Oh, he's probably daid, the house caved in.'

"And then he comes out just in time and he looks in your face!

"Right then you feel he's supposed to kill you. You know what you'd do if somebody left you in a burning house. Right then you feel he's supposed to hate you because he would have a right to hate you. And he says, 'Man, why didn't you wake me up? Why did you let me stay in that house? THE HOUSE WAS ON FIRE! MAN, YOU WERE GONNA LET ME BURN! WHAT'S THE TROUBLE WITH YOU, BUB?'

"Right then you'd take the defense. You'd say, 'I didn't know, I didn't mean it. Don't kill me!' You feel like he *might* kill you.

"Well, that's what white Americans are like. The house's been on fire for three hundred and ten years and the whites have let the blacks sleep" Muhammed Ali (Olsen, p. 110).

In this parable, Muhammed Ali gives voice to the resentment and feelings of betrayal that are providing the rationale of separatism for the Black Muslims and many other militant groups. Two images recur in black tales, that of a fire and that of blacks sleeping while being exploited and subordinated.

> Well, of course, they always tell the story about St. Peter's touring heaven showing one of the whites heaven, who had just arrived, and they were going on this tour and of course when they got to one section of town he told the man to "Let's tiptoe now, we have to be very quiet, this is where the Negroes live, and you know this is Saturday night, and we don't want to wake them up." [58]

———

> Then there was the story of the southern white man who went to the train station to meet his northern white friend who came down, and sitting there at the train station, at least, on the porch of the old station were two Negroes, one was asleep, one was reading a paper, however the paper was upside down. So when the two men left the train station the Southerner kicked the one reading the paper, and the Northerner said, "Would you please explain that? I don't understand it. I would think that if you were going to kick one you would kick the lazy one who's sleeping." The Southerner said, "that's not the one we're worried about." [59]

This chapter will review the rhetoric of the awakers and the awakeners, assessing the direction and force of those who are actively seeking identity from within the black cultural resources.

Negroes have commonly been regarded as a minority group. But since their relationship to the majority group and its culture is so different from that of most other minority groups, the very definition of minorities is called into question. The element that ties together the individuals within other groups—such as Jews, Italians, and Mexican-Americans—seems notably lacking among Negroes, that is, a sense of cultural identity distinct from that of the dominant culture. These other groups exhibit a sense of being threatened by the culture of the majority. They express this, at least at first, by clinging to characteristics that emphasize this cultural distinctness. Further, as we have seen with Mexican-Americans, they develop (or develop upon) stereotypes of the individuals in the outside group, the very ones who are surrounding and besieging him. This is the primary attribute of the characteristic minority member: he sees himself besieged, hemmed-in, his cultural existence imperilled. He is on the inside, keeping the invaders and the despoilers out. But blacks, in accepting the white stereotype and the American Dream, commonly see themselves as outsiders waiting to get in.

This does not mean that there has been a total definition of self in terms of white man's values and life style. It has become evident in recent sociological surveys that the point made in the joke in which the Negro wipes his ass on the American flag that the Negroes have no pride in their "place," no historical and cultural roots to rely upon, and little self-confidence in their present life style is bringing about a reaction in the man in the street. This reaction calls not only for the defiant gesture but also for the fabrication of roots—by learning African history and Swahili and by adopting certain West African modes of dress—and by forming a Black Nation here. Those who are working in the ghettos report that "nine out of every ten youngsters in Harlem are now black nationalists" and further that "nationalism comes in a variety of brands, ranging from a positive identification with Afro-American history and culture, to the more racist varieties that call for separation . . ." (Duberman).

DEVIANTS

Such a position, while it emphasizes the major ways in which Negroes differ from most ethnic minorities, moves Negroes who feel this way into the position not of membership in an assimilatable minority but rather into the position of deviants—those who are branded by majority culture as acting in an abnormal or anti-normative fashion.

Deviants, when they form communities, define themselves in terms of mainstream culture and how they differ from it, not in terms of how intrinsically different they are, as minorities do. In other words, deviant communities look on the culture of dominant society as wrong, and define themselves by trying to up-end the values and characteristic activities of the dominant group. Most minorities, on the other hand, make no attempt either to bring about change or to argue against the culture surrounding them. They do not understand the others, and thus fear them, defensively cohering in the face of the threat of a cultural dominance that in most cases will bring about assimilation anyhow, at least those minorities that are enclaved in the city. Both minorities and deviant groups are defined in terms of disparity from dominant culture, but deviants work offensively, challenging the presuppositions of the majority, while minorities seem to ask simply to be left alone.

This image of Negroes as deviants is implicitly recognized by many members of deviant groups. For instance, the argot developed by many outsider groups is self-consciously derived from the Negro musician's slang, variously called "jazz talk," "jiving," or "hip talk." Enough vocabulary is derived from this common source to make an argument that there is a *lingua franca* of many deviant communities. But this identification goes beyond vocabulary in these same groups to the area of life style. Hippies and other recent Bohemian groups have openly proclaimed themselves "white niggers" by which they seem to mean that, like blacks, they represent an alternative to the life style of majority-group American culture. By this, they attempt to define *themselves* but do little for the definition of the culture of blackness.

Ultimately, attitudes and practices of the members of these deviant communities are practices not so much in emulation of blacks but a rejection of their own cultural heritage and value-system. Dirtiness, sexual promiscuity, thievery, and other characteristics common to most of these deviant groups are the most direct means of attacking the world whose highest proclaimed values are honesty, cleanliness, and sexual continence. The fact that these hostile characteristics are also purported to be true of blacks gives the deviant a group to which he can point as living "the true life." But this stereotypes the Negro just as much as the majority group from which he is reacting. In a sense, it is accepting the black's vision of these traits as good ones, but as we have seen, this does little to dispel the stereotyped notions. And there is a difference between blacks and deviants which is remarked upon in the current anecdote about a Negro talking with a hippie, in which the former says "Oh man, all you need to do is go home and wash your face." The deviant has the choice of whether he will stand outside mainstream culture; the black, like a minority group member, has had no alternative. The deviant steps into the outsider role; the Negro is type-cast there by the "director."

The deviant's rhetoric announces that he has been an insider, but he wants *out*; the Negro has proclaimed for the last fifty years, and especially during the civil rights movement of the fifties and sixties, that he has been excluded always and that now he wants *in*. But the failure of the integration movement to allay the identity problems of Negroes and of black communities has resulted in a shift of tactics. The rhetoric of blackness is an openly defiant stance which makes those who take this position share even more with deviant groups.

If the riots have done nothing else, they have forced a taking of sides and they have dramatized aggressive alternatives which have been more meaningful to the black man-on-the-street than the sit-ins and the marches ever were. The riots according to the most recent reports have galvanized the opinions of the black man in the cities into a vaguely articulated but nonetheless real agreement with the aims of Black Power and Black Nationalism (Beardwood, 1967). Such separatist groups are therefore presented with the possibility of massive backing in the development of programs that underline the importance and dignity of being a black human being.

SOUL

The slogan of this movement, "Black is Beautiful," emphasizes the point made earlier that life is often envisaged in esthetic terms and therefore performers and good performances are highly valued. This point is significant in terms of my argument, not just because it illuminates an area of black-white cultural disparity, but because the concept of "soul" around which one sees the beginnings of a black group identity being forged is also derived from a descriptive esthetic term first applied to a style of music.

Central to an understanding of "soul" is knowing what it means in musical terms and how it differs from black music of the past. Soul is essentially a performance term—a singer may have soul but specific songs do not—which arose as a number of traditional Negro styles came together. Beginning around 1955 there was a resurgence of a number of older traditional sounds in Negro popular music: country blues, classic blues, and gospel. A group of musicians centering on Horace Silver and Art Blakely and Ray Charles brought together, through a solid sense of musicianship and a wide grasp of styles, the sacred and the secular sounds of gospel and blues. This meant the introduction of a certain amount of the religious type call-and-response pattern into blues-type songs and a utilization of religious emotional fervor for secular purposes. For a time the terms "roots," "hard-bop," and "funky" vied with "soul" for the name of this new movement, but the latter has assumed control since about 1960 (Szwed). This is fitting because of the continuing role of the gospel sound and the importance of church singers such as Mahalia Jackson and more recently Aretha Franklin in the fashioning of the soul sound. But such church music is only one of the traditional styles contributing to this sound, and in many ways not as important as the country and street blues.

The fifties witnessed a rediscovery of the old street blues approach. As Leroi Jones pointed out:

> By the time the large dance and show bands started to develop into jazz bands, the more autonomous blues forms had gone largely underground, had returned, as it was to be enjoyed by the *subculture* in which they were most functional as a collective expression. At house parties and all-black cabarets and clubs, the blues was almost always still in evidence. And not only the newer city, or urban, blues held complete sway, although it was the most contemporary expression for a great many Negroes in the "colored sections" of the North and Midwest, but the older country blues was heard wherever there were people who knew and loved it best (Jones, 1963, p. 166).

When the blues came back into popularity, however, the country styles of the street singers were strongly altered to bring them in line with other performance styles which had been popular in the meanwhile, the rhythm and blues and the classic blues traditions, both of which carried an instrumental ensemble behind the singer. The audience was highly conscious of the roots of this kind of music, but they were also cognizant of the changes being made. The "down home" sound was not greatly appreciated—whenever I would play a recording of an old-time blues performer for my Philadelphia friends they would begin to giggle. One of Charles Keil's city informants explains the difference between country blues and the more recent and approved styles in this way: "They're mellow, man. None of that gutbucket stuff, you know . . . they've refined it, so it's smooth and easy—no harps, moaning, or shit like that. These guys have brought the blues up to date—made it modern" (Keil, p. 157).

Though Blakey and Silver spearheaded the movement, it was the working singers of the fifties who actually wrought the change of taste in the popular audience, singers such as Ray Charles, B. B. King, Jimmy Reed, Bobby "Blue" Bland. These performers all came from some branch of the blues tree. Most of them play their own instrumental background and write a great deal of their own material. Furthermore, most of their songs (with the exception of Charles) are in 12-bar blues form and style; however some break this up with an occasional four line stanza that functions something like the "channel" or "bridge" of the pop ballad. But the performance has been severely affected by the "Rhythm and Blues" style of the forties in which the singer performs over an ensemble which functions primarily as a rhythmic unit or to provide a response to the singer's call.

Throughout the fifties and early sixties these singers from an essentially individual-performer blues tradition were adapting themselves to performing with a group, and developing their style into a "show" format. This meant a certain amount of experimentation before the show-pattern asserted itself, experimentation both in the area of presentation and of songs. The singer, Bo Diddley, is in some ways the most representative, and in other ways the most unusual of these transitional blues performers. One of the earliest to achieve wide popularity, he wrote songs not only in the country blues pattern but also went to a number of other traditional Negro performance types for the substance of his material. In fact, the "Bo Diddley sound," a biting rhythm on the pattern is most directly taken from the routine of "Hambone," a male adolescent handclapping and chanting rhythmic piece which is widely found throughout the United States, and which has a complicated performance history.*

In the "Hambone" routine, there is an alternation between a chanted line and the rhythmic clapping. One line is droned out and is then answered by clapping of approximately the same duration. Sometimes after a verse is ended, the boys will improvise at great length on the basic rhythm, not only by clapping but slapping legs, arms, shoulders, tables, or anything handy. This can go on indefinitely until someone shouts "Hambone!" Hambone becomes a character, and his exploits make him something of a hard-man.

> Hambone went to the grocer's store.
> Shit on the counter and pissed on the floor.
> Hambone said he don't give a damn.
> He'll wipe his ass with a piece of ham. [60]

But the routine most commonly calls for an improvisation on the pattern of:

> Hambone, Hambone have you heard?
> Poppa's gonna buy you a mockingbird.
> If that mockingbird don't sing,
> Poppa's gonna buy you a diamond ring.
> If that diamond ring don't shine,
> Poppa's gonna buy you a bottle of wine.
> If that bottle of wine gets broke,

---

* The routine of "Hambone" seems to have started with shoeshine boys imitating the sounds of bones players (who themselves were imitating tap-dancers). Minstrel stage origins of the routine are strongly implied because the common verse "Hambone walk, Hambone talk, Hambone eat with a knife and fork" derives from the piece called "Juba" or "Walk, Jawbone, Walk." The polymetric clapping technique itself, however, with the insistent variety of tone textures, is observably an African retention.

Poppa's gonna buy you a billy goat.
If that billy goat runs away,
Poppa's gonna buy you a stack of hay.
If that stack of hay gets wet,
Poppa's gonna beat your butt I bet. [60]

Bo Diddley uses this routine as his signature, using his own name rather than "Hambone." He also returns to it repeatedly for inspiration, uniting it with other traditional pieces. In addition to his only slightly revised version of the traditional piece, recorded as "Hush Your Mouth," he has a piece called simply "Bo Diddley."

Bo Diddley buy his baby a diamond ring.
If that diamond ring don't shine,
He gonna take it to a private eye.
If that private eye can't see,
He better not take that ring from me.

Bo Diddley caught a nanny goat
To make his pretty baby a Sunday coat.
Bo Diddley caught a bearcat
To make his pretty baby a Sunday hat. [61]

It was blues men like Bo Diddley, B. B. King, Bobby Bland, and Ray Charles who brought about the development of blues into soul, through being willing to return and take a new look at their black heritage in this way. These are still blues men in that they still sing songs in blues style, and they still live the transient life of the old blues singers (though they no longer have to perform on the streets) (Keil, pp. 143–63). However, except for Ray Charles, these performers have not been the ones to reap the rewards of defining soul, nor of bringing this music to the attention of the world. This has been done by Otis Redding, Ray Charles, Wilson Pickett, James Brown, Aretha Franklin, and the other recording stars of the sixties. These more recent singers have not so much the country blues background as a grounding in the classic blues. This is clearly seen in the work of Ray Charles, who found his characteristic sound through the work of early piano men like Jimmy Yancey, Speckled Red, and

Jelly Roll Morton; this derivation is also clear with Aretha Franklin whose songs (and, to some extent, approach) are in the tradition of singers like Ma Rainey, Ida Cox, and Bessie Smith.

This discussion emphasizes that there is an historical and cultural continuity between blues and soul music. However, as Keil has demonstrated, there is a major difference both in content and strategy of the songs in these styles; this difference can probably best be described as one in which blues argue "I'm lonesome—let's get together" while soul explores "let's see how we can stay together." Both "blues" and "soul" are emotional affect words as well as names for singing styles; but the emotions differ. The blues emotion is concerned with feelings of alienation, and thus, by extension, blues songs are ones that describe states and feelings arising from the alienated and rootless situation. Having soul, on the other hand, is a communal emotion, and soul songs argue for attempts at interpersonal reconciliations, with the facts of life always borne in mind. Both types of songs are hard-headed, honest, and realistic in their content, but blues rest on a base of essential loneliness because of the way life is, while soul songs tell how to learn to stay together in spite of (or by accepting) the way things are. Both articulate the conflict of the sexes, the blues emphasizing the coming together, the parting, the loneliness, the soul songs tending to focus on the strains and strengths and beauty of being together.

A typical blues song takes the theme of alienation and embodies it in a series of images or reflections revolving around this theme. Here, for instance, is a song by the early city bluesman, Big Bill Broonzy, called "Sun Gonna Shine in My Door."

> Just sitting here hungry, ain't got a dime,
> Looks like my friends would come to see me some time,
> But it won't matter how it happens,
> The sun gonna shine in my door someday.

> When I was in jail, expectin' a fine,
> When I went before that judge, not a friend could I find,
> But it won't matter how it happens
> The sun gonna shine in my door someday.

I lost my father, lost brother too,
That's why you hear me singin', I'm lonesome and blue,
But it don't matter how it happens
The sun gonna shine in my door someday.

Lawdy, lawdy, lawdy, lawd,
I used to be your reg'lar, now I got to be your dog,
But it won't matter how it happens
The sun gonna shine in my door someday.

I'm in trouble, no one to pay my fine,
When I get out this time, gonna leave this town a-flyin',
But it won't matter how it happens
The sun gonna shine in my door someday.

I was with my buddy, through thick and thin,
My buddy got away and I got in,
But it won't matter how it happens
The sun gonna shine in my door someday. [62]

The focus of such songs seems to be on the accumulation of experiences, all leading to the same feeling of being lost and alone. The address is to an audience that has been through the same kind of experiences. The I-You relationship is commonly between the singer and the audience, and if a specific person is referred to, the pronoun used will be "he" or "she." Repeatedly, a blues song begins with a direct address to the audience:

Did you ever, did you ever wake up and find your baby gone?
You were so disappointed until you cried all day long.

or:

Listen folks, it's no joke
I'm as blue as I can be.

The classic blues differ somewhat from the country blues in their approach. While the typical country blues say "Look what we've all been through," by sharing experiences with the audience, the classic blues more commonly say, "This is the kind of scene we go through all of the time." There is, in other words, more of a sense of on-going experience in the classic blues. The I-You relationship is more often one between two characters in a scene depicted in the song. The impression given is that a scene is being overheard, such as when Lil Green begins a song:

> In the dark, it's just you and I
> Not a sound, there's not one sigh,
> Just a beat of my heart
> In the dark. [63]

or when Bessie Smith sings "Judge, judge, dear kind judge, send me to the 'lectric chair."

This "overheard scene" technique has been borrowed and developed upon in the soul repertoire. It is characteristic of the songs of most of the great soul singers, even one like B. B. King, who derives from the country and city blues traditions. Bobby Bland, who has now dropped the "Blue" from his name to signify his changing of styles, also directs nearly all of his songs to a fictional "you," most commonly a woman. And to indicate his changeover, to the bluesman who says that blues are all round him and there is no way of getting away from them Bland proposes:

> You needn't be lonely, you shouldn't be blue,
> I'll design a life of love for you.

This message of conciliation is underlined by the performance pattern of soul singers. Whereas the city bluesman, like his country counterpart, emphasized his isolation by singing to his own accompaniment (often speaking to his guitar or piano as a friend), the soul singer is involved in a show in which he is the coordinator of an ensemble. His role is one of leader as well as comforter. He argues from a position of strength through numbers rather than weakness and isolation.

This is not to argue that interpersonal, and especially intersexual conflict is a problem of the past. Soul songs as well as blues articulate the troubles involved in people needing to live together and yet being driven apart by internal and external forces. But soul songs often provide strategies for articulating these conflicts and proclaim the possibility of a future, of a continuing relationship through satisfaction (emotional, sexual, financial) and mutual pleasure.

"Soul" has a sexual dimension to its meanings, like most Negro terms for musical styles such as "jazz," "rock and roll," "boogie-woogie" (as in "I wonder who's boogieing my woogie now"), and "funky." Soul has, among other meanings, become a euphemism for sexual drive, as in Jelly Roll Morton's boasting song, "Roll, Mr. Jelly" where he sings:

> They call me Mr. Jelly
> You sure know how to roll.
> You got rockin', rockin' rhythm
> That satisfies my soul. [45]

Typically, the strategy of many soul songs calls for one partner to satisfy the other—"Sock it to me," "Yeah, baby, whip it to me when you get home"—or has the singer promising the kinds of pleasures that will keep the other coming back for more. And soul, even as it has accrued social meanings far beyond the musical context, has kept this sexual honesty as part of its field of meaning.

This note of honesty, of "telling it how it is," in song has become one of the central features of the concept of soul as it has broadened from the interpersonal to the intercultural sphere of life. But the concept has broadened primarily by a recognition by Negroes that the essence of the difference between blacks and whites is in their patterns of performance. Not only does black song reject the moon-June type of dishonesty, but black singers recognize, as a culturally distinctive feature, their need to have total identification of both singer and audience with performance. A black singer must have an audience to support him, and his greatest performances are therefore "live"—as opposed to many of the most influential white "rock" musicians who have gravitated more and more away from concerts and dances to studio production of records. As one soul song self-consciously expresses, soul means participation:

If you feel like singing
If you feel like dancing
Then this record has soul.

Soul has become a word in which this concept of group involve-
ment in the esthetic experience, and honesty, has been broadened
from the entertainment arena into other social areas. As early as
1960, John Szwed was pointing out that

> If soul were merely a musical phenomenon it would be inter-
> esting enough, but it has accompanying aspects that extend
> deeply into race consciousness and strong anti-white sentiments
> (Szwed, p. 360).

Soul has not only provided an emotional and conceptual focus for
Negro musical developments but also it has become a rallying cry
for a black social movement which uses the concept as an aggressive
device, part of the elaborate "hidden language," bringing Negroes
together and excluding whites.

This aggressive use of music and related expressive forms has been
a part of black life since slavery. It has become more virulent lately
as black musicians have realized that not only has the aggression
gone unrecognized by whites, but that white musicians have consistently taken over black expressive styles because of their energetic,
liberating qualities. The reaction on the part of some avant-garde
Negro jazz players, like Thelonus Monk and Miles Davis, has been
to attempt to produce a more and more esoteric sound in order to
leave the white audience behind: they present their music as aggression. For instance, *Time* Magazine says of Miles, "on stage, he
storms inwardly, glaring at his audience, wincing at his trumpet,
stabbing and tugging at his ear. Often his solos degenerate into a
curse blown again and again . . . he still creates a mood of terror
suppressed." The problem with this approach is that, except for the
very few musical geniuses who follow this course, there are few who
can adhere to its demanding ways, and the audience, even in Negro
communities, is very limited.

The development of the soul sound was an attempt to do the
same kind of aggressing but in a more public vocabulary. But going

to the roots sound, the Negro performer rediscovered a style which, among other things, he felt the whites would be incapable of copying and debasing; he also found a large enough audience among blacks (and only more recently urban whites) to keep the movement going. Thus, "the step from *cool* to *soul*" as Leroi Jones has shown, "is a form of social aggression."

> It is an attempt to place upon a meaningless social order, an order which would give value to terms of existence that were once considered not only valueless but shameful. *Cool* means non-participation; *soul* means a new establishment. It is an attempt to reverse the social roles within the society by redefining the canons of value. . . . 'soul brother' means to recast the social order in its own image. White is then not 'right,' as the old blues have it, but a liability, since the culture of white precludes the possession of a Negro 'soul' (Jones, 1963, p. 219; *see* Szwed, p. 365).

The extension of the term "soul" from musical style to life-style has therefore meant that an aggressive device developed by musicians became effective in other realms of experience. Thus there has been a parallel development of terms like "soul brother" and "soul food," both harking back to elements of Negro life that are irretrievably Negro, and indeed part of those very elements of Negro life focussed on by the white stereotype. "Soul brother" certainly derives, with many aspects of soul music, from Negro religious style; "Soul" in the religious sense is self-apparent, but with "brother" we see a church becoming the institutional model for the cooperative life. The clearest manifestation of this cooperation is the use of the terms "brother" and "sister" for members of one's church. "Soul food," the chit'lin's, hog maw, and collard greens which came North with the immigrations, so long the butt of jokes concerning Negroes, becomes one of the rallying points in the establishment of a black identity. Dick Gregory's comment on the use of this food in an aggressive context has become part of the oral traditions of the city Negro, especially the Black Nationalist and the Civil Rights worker.

> Well, Dick Gregory always tells the story that he sit in for eleven months to get the restaurants to open up and when they finally opened

they didn't have what he wanted on the menu. What he wanted was some chit'lins, collard greens, and potatoes. [64]

In the concept of "soul," then, we see a willingness to accept elements of the unpleasant past of the black American experience—in the glorification of the cast-off type of food and the accommodating "better bye 'n' bye" religion (or at least, its emotional and spiritual by-products). What the "soul strategists" are doing, Keil points out, is attempting "to turn old liabilities into new assets."

The term "soul" begins as a descriptive concept, but in becoming associated with blackness and the aspirations of blacks, changes to a term of appraisal. Further, it is not only "soul *sounds*" that are beautiful but anything else that exhibits soul. The concept is therefore another, and perhaps the best, example of esthetic terminology being extended into the realm of ethics, where "beautiful" becomes "good" and "ugly" means "bad." This element is emphasized because the point of soul seems to be that the emotional, esthetic experience from which the term derives can serve as the model for what blacks share and, even more important, *how* they can share it.

ROMANTIC NATIONALISM

The use of *soul* in such a context of unity through discovering group roots, through perceiving the common enemy, and through a growing emphasis on how black and white differ from each other, is not totally an unknown or unrecognizable use of the term. It is the very use set forth by the adherents of Romantic Nationalism, who have been so important in providing the rationale for the struggle for "self-determination" of so many nations created in the nineteenth and twentieth centuries.

In fact, all of the terms associated with the "soul" movement have similar echoes. We see with the use of the word "brother" the establishment of the requisite sense of brotherhood in battle, a sense further underlined by the recent synonyms for "brother": "blood," "members," and "people" (as in "he's a 'people'"). It therefore seems useful to review the tenets of Romantic Nationalism as proposed by

Herder and his followers to see how much of that philosophy is shared by the "soul movement." *

Nationalism is a state of mind calling for the subordinating of an individual to the interest of his nation-state. It is, like patriotism, often an irrational, indeed anti-rational approach to the development of units of government based on geographical, cultural, and/or linguistic sharing. But this does not mean that all nationalistic movements have been anti-rational. Indeed both the American and French nationalistic revolutions announced programs of government based on the utopian ideals proposed during the Enlightenment, and fought against the tyrannies of authoritarian (i.e. unenlightened, coercive) states.

In the French and American Revolutions there was no attempt to realign political boundaries to conform to the outlines of language or culture areas; rather they wished to provide new methods of governing nations which already had a feeling of statehood. This was not true of the Central and Eastern European movements of the nineteenth century, for they were dealing with much less stable national situations—ones in which coercion came from without rather than from within. In such cases, nationalism "became a movement not so much to protect against the injustices of an authoritarian state but an attempt to redraw political boundaries to fit the contour of ethnic bodies. . . . In contradistinction to liberal nationalism, romantic nationalism emphasized passion and instinct instead of reason, national differences instead of common aspirations, and above all, the building of nations on the traditions and myths of the past . . . instead of on political realities of the present" (Wilson, p. 3).

The major difference, then, is much like the differences in the Civil Rights and black militant movements here—the former arguing against the authoritarian elements within the social and political systems of which they are a part, the latter proclaiming themselves a people apart and seeing the coercion coming from without, from a system in which they have never had a place.

---

* Throughout this discussion, my argument is indebted to the convenient survey of Romantic Nationalism proposed by William A. Wilson.

The rationale of Romantic Nationalism turns on the idea of national character or *national soul*. Herder described this idea in an extended metaphor:

> As the mineral water derives its component parts, its operative power, and its flaws from the soil through which it flows, so the ancient characteristics of peoples arose from the family features, the climate, the way of life and education (tradition) the early actions and employments, that were peculiar to them. The manners of the fathers took deep root and became the internal prototypes of the descendants (Wilson, p. 5).

The use of "soul" in black parlance drives in this same direction, toward a sense of ethnic unity based on some innate, irrational sense of community, brotherhood. Further, the meanings of soul hark back to the heritage of the Southern experience since this is what is shared by all members of the group. Of course, there is a selection of traits from Southern life: strong distinction from whites, revivalistic-type religious experiences and the sense of unity stemming from them; the communality of life lived in the church; and Southern cooking. The most important use of separatism will be to allow for the development of a black identity based on black culture, an aim that echoes the call of Romantic Nationalism for ethnic peoples to develop in accord with their own innate abilities, in line with their own culture pattern (Wilson, p. 6).

One of the major problems in developing a black identity is in finding cultural roots. To be sure, the Southern experience has provided some of the salient features for this development, but this was the very place in which culture was stripped from the Africans. Therefore, there can only be a strong sense of ambivalence about using the culture and milieu of the black South as a model on which to build. This ambivalence is undoubtedly one reason for the attempt to go back even farther in black history and cultural experience, back as far as Africa. But, for the moment, this is doomed to a similar failure since American Negroes know so little of Africa and not all they know can they identify with. The affecting of "African" clothing and hair-styles and the need to speak Swahili fail to recognize that these are not Pan-African cultural elements but traits tied to a limited number of African groups.

However, Romantic Nationalism does not demand cultural truth or validity, but culturally-derived symbols around which the people may rally. It is a philosophy or point of view, not an education system; it is not so much oriented toward recapturing the past as toward providing an image that will allow the capturing of the future. And the only way this can happen, this line of thought seems to say, is by developing a *cultural* identity on which individual identities can then be based.

REVITALIZATION

Romantic Nationalism is essentially a rhetorical position, but out of it have grown many new nations and self-sufficient cultural enclaves. There is a gulf, however, between the proclamation of this position and acting on its precepts. The riots, as pointed out above, are not in themselves actions of this sort, since they apparently occurred before these ideas had gained any wide acceptance among street-people. But what seems important to note is that the "soul" ideal has come to be more widely accepted as a rationale for such activity by both rioters and observers (militant and otherwise); thus the separatist argument is used more widely today than before the riots. What we may see is the beginnings of what is known to anthropologists as a "revitalization movement."

> Very commonly revitalization movements occur in societies, or groups within societies, which perceive themselves to be locked in a peculiar dilemma. Such dilemmas are apt to occur in acculturation situations, in international politics, and in situations of factionalism within a single society. . . . This dilemma can only be solved, as long as the identity preferences of the group preclude its alliance with [a group regarded as "the enemy"], by a revitalization movement which redefines the situation. This redefinition must include a new image of the group which is so satisfying, in a nativistic sense, that the group is confident of its ability to "go it alone," without identification or alliances with . . . other . . . groups . . . the revitalization movement is the

process by which an extremely disorganized society accomplishes the task of reorganization (Wallace, pp. 212–13, 214).*

Charles Keil has suggested that the Black Muslim ideology conforms to that of the classic revitalization pattern (Keil, p. 186). He refers to their formulation of a code of behavior, a preaching of the code, and the creation of an organization to enforce and propagate the code. In this regard, the Black Muslims do indeed come closest to the usual operation of the revitalization process. But it appears that the Black Muslims have not grown; rather the black power movement is still searching for its prophet who will articulate the code and who will build the organization. The only element lacking, seemingly, is a truly charismatic leader (or set of leaders) who will enlist wide popular support and show the man-in-the-street the proper way to black identity.

Perhaps the most important feature of resemblance between revitalization movements and the present separatist position is that both turn on the idea of social and cultural polarization within a pluralistic situation. Just as these Negroes now insist that they be called blacks and that "black is beautiful," all but one of the varieties of revitalization movements which Wallace outlines call for a recognition and an expulsion of "the others." Since the present situation shares some elements of these varieties of revitalization, it seems useful to note them here. They are:

> Revivalistic, which aims to restore a golden age believed to have existed in the society's past and which ignores or expels the alien group; utopian, which aims to achieve a golden age believed to lie in the future, but to be implicit in the evolving patterns of the present, and which also ignores or expels the alien group; assimilative, which aims to import many of the customs of the alien [usually dominant] group, to combine them syncretistically with

---

* I have, in giving this quotation, emphasized those elements of the Negro situation which fit into Wallace's definition of revitalization movements. It is necessary to point out that the classic situation for such a development is not fulfilled here—a situation in which the disorganized group has its identity crisis intensified because it is caught between *two* other groups, identifying with the values of one to the exclusion of those of the other whom it considers the enemy.

native customs of the alien group and to dissolve social boundaries between the two societies; and *expropriative*, which aims to import many of the customs of the alien group and to combine them with native customs, but to expel alien persons (Wallace, p. 165).

MIDDLE-CLASS CONVERTS

It is difficult to determine at this point whether blacks are rallying to the cry of "soul" and entering a revitalistic phase or whether we simply are observing the exhibitions of the rhetorical dimension of a period of Romantic Nationalism. There is one important indication that there is more than just a verbal pose involved; the black middle class, which has previously identified itself with white values and institutions, have given indications that they are being won over to the cause.

> "At the start of the riots, the black middle class didn't want any part of it. As things got hot, some of the police took potshots at those good, smug, middle class houses, where the people were sitting around the television, disapproving of all those blacks destroying property. And suddenly, those middle-class people woke up. They know that even though they were making money, and living well, and talking cultured, they were no different." [65]

> "When they start talking about Negroes, I say I'm a Negro too," says Leon Coward, fifty-two, director of a Day Care Center in New York City. "But my brother down there, he could kick me in the pants, 'cause he knows I've got a bellyful, and his is empty. Now we're getting to the point where I am beginning to recognize this man's empty belly." (Beardwood, pp. 149, 151)*

Paralleling this changeover in middle-class attitudes have been a number of jokes that have ridiculed the assimilationist tendencies of upward-mobile Negroes. These have been especially current among Civil Rights workers and other middle-class, but involved, Negroes

* Reprinted by permission of Fortune Magazine © 1967 Fortune Magazine.

to whom identity loss is a real danger. They have therefore operated primarily as a social control mechanism and only secondarily as an indicator of social friction and stratification.*

Did you hear about the Negro woman and her son who moved into the white neighborhood? They were the very first Negro family to move in, and you know what that means. They had bricks thrown at them, their epitaphs written on the sidewalks, and all sorts of things like that. They really went through hell, but they never flinched; just about everything you can image. Well after they had been there a few months and had gone through all this hell, one day the woman was at the window and suddenly said, "Oh, Lord, I guess we better start packing." The boy asked why. The woman answers, "One of *them* is moving in!" [66]

————

This old Negro man had worked for this white, you know, white-dominated company for years, and years, and years. And he had become, you know, the only Negro there and was accustomed to being around white people that he never thought of himself as a Negro or anything; he had lost all identity. And so he got on a bus, and he was going home from work one day, and he climbed on the bus and it was real crowded and there wasn't any place to sit, except next to this one old white woman. He saw the seat and he sat down on the bus. The woman looked up very shocked and says, "There's colored people on this bus." And he got up and looked around and he said, "Where! Where! Where!?" [67]

————

That reminds me of one I heard about this Negro was out hitch-hiking one day and this white fellow passed in a truck and he say, "Say, would you like a ride," and he says, "Yes." And the white fellow pulled out his lunch, and he said, "Would you like to have half of this sand-

* Many of the same jokes are told by whites (usually liberals) where they serve a very different purpose.

wich?" And he said, "Yes." And he gave him half of the san, he said, "You want me to eat half of your sandwich?" He said, "Yea." He said, "Would you like to drink some soda water?" He said, "You mean drink soda water, out of the same bottle that you?" So they got so friendly there until finally they had a flat tire, and they went out to check the flat tire and this man said that, "I bet we not gonna be able to get any help to fix this tire." And the fellow said, "Yeah, I bet we won't be able to find a nigger anywhere." [68]

SOUL IS SASS

The vocabulary of "soul," the riots, the developments on campuses and among the Black Panthers are proclaiming anything but unison. But it is not by chance that they are arising at about the same time. There *is* a voice coming from within the Negro community hesitantly proclaiming a sense of identity, asserting power in its own language and cadences. If this seems to whites to be a language that they have known for a long time, the esoteric strategy and vocabulary of "soul" must be proclaimed even louder, for it is a language which is more natural and self-confident, and more strident than ever heard before from blacks. Even if the kinds of activity seem reminiscent of the stereotypical Negro, the actions are more positive in proclaiming the beauty of being black. As a Watts rioter said:

"Man, let me tell you, it was wild! And if they don't stop fucking with us, we gonna burn some more! That's right, baby! We *got some soul*, now!" (Conot, p. 361).

And now black intellectuals are asking *themselves* what "soul" is, and the answer is cultural identity, distinctive style which can lead to self-respect. It is being Negro and acting like one without being ashamed to act in this way. What is soul?

Soul is sass, man. Soul is arrogance. Soul is walkin' down the street in a way that says, "This is me, muh-fuh!" Soul is that nigger whore comin' along . . . ja . . . ja . . . ja, and walkin' like she's sayin', "Here it is, baby. Come an' git it." Soul is bein' true to yourself, to what is *you*. Now, hold on: soul . . . that . . . uninhibited . . . no, *extremely* un-inhibited self . . . expression that goes into practically every Negro endeavor. That's soul. And there's swagger in it, man. It's exhibitionism, and it's effortless. Effortless. You don't need to put it on; it just comes out. (Claude Brown) *

Soul then, which began as a search for roots, has gravitated toward an expression of an entire world view, one which emphasizes cultural integrity—honesty in expression, in feeling, especially in not being afraid to perform publicly in the way in which the spirit strikes. Soul *is* sass. It is, if nothing else, a rhetoric of on-going confrontation. Soul is an attitude which allows a black to look Whitey straight in the eye and say,

"This is me, motherfucker, whatcha gonna do about it?" or "Now it's just me and you, Fu Manchu!"

Soul is a willingness to stand up and speak out. It is a need *not* to be counted but to be counting; an exhibition of oneself as sharing in the on-going process of life by releasing an energy which comes from without even as it seems to well forth from within. Soul is shared and sharing energy and performance; its mode of presentation is the *going on* and not the winning of the victory, the prize.

This discourse system is a product of the lower-class black, I've been arguing. But in a real sense this does violence to performances, and represents a white point of view. For it isn't accurate to look at the material as a *product* of anything but rather as part of a *process* of living. Furthermore, though the stories and the songs may arise from the ghettoes, it is becoming more and more evident that other blacks, especially college students and militants, are borrowing ghetto rhetoric, the strategy of confrontation.

In the uprisings on campuses we witness an exhibition of soul-brothering in the *deliberate* use of street-style rapping. The vocabulary of attack is all there; no more big nouns in the center of these confrontations, only words that move. To the white charge that it is all talk, *just* rhetoric, the answer is that it's not talk but talk*ing*. It is "throwing a rap" at the others, asking for a response in kind. It is process talk, in which someone "caps" on another, "charging," "mounting," "running it out." Just as rapping to a "fox"

* Reprinted by permission of *Esquire* Magazine, © 1968 by Esquire, Inc.

(good-looking girl) is not expressed as a "line" but "putting her through the changes," so rapping with administrators calls for a similar coercive but reciprocal activity. This is true whenever blacks are talking to "the man" but this goes unrecognized, for in such matters, the man is "lame." Blacks who know "where it's at," who have "gotten into it" are "fast, fast, fast." The man in his lameness is "slow, slow, slow."

But these words don't stand alone. They are part of a world view which sees life as an on-going expression of energy through confrontation and willingness to coerce and be coerced. This is certainly behind the "demands" of black students throughout the country. And it is perhaps the saddest part of the black-white struggle, for in the open confrontation there seems to be the greatest amount of misunderstanding.

> *College administrators, the police, the American public see these demands—in horse race terms—as contests which can be won or lost. They see them, in other words, as set battle-pieces that might be recorded in the history books. Thus, there is a feeling that the specific demands must be met or rejected. Either resolution is frustrating to the blacks, for winning or losing is an end to the confrontation, and by extension, an end to the establishment's acknowledgment of the black presence which accorded them the sense of place that was really the heart of their demands.*

To the demand that the blacks be given a forum wherein they may be heard on a continuing basis, the institutional powers reply "that is a luxury we cannot afford. It takes up too much of our time." What is really meant is that the open acknowledgment of coercion and counter-coercion is an embarrassment when performed so loudly, so publicly.

We can see this cultural gap most fully in the ways in which that "very O.K." word, *dialogue* has been used lately. Intended as a term for on-going discussion between individuals or groups in contention, it has come to be almost synonymous with "ventilation" and "compromise." In other words, the frame of reference in which one looks

for closure, for tension and relief, for problem and solution, for conflict and resolution. Because of the embarassment of publicity, the
quicker the resolution, the better. And then one can look with pride
at compromise, as a thing which has been hammered out, and its
very "thing-ness" gives a sense of satisfaction. End of discussion:
Great surprise and disgust when the feeling of tension remains!

The conflict-resolution pattern is fundamental to esthetics and
ethics that are based on a balanced image of life. In the most
threatening situations we resort to our most extreme technique for
bringing relief as quickly as possible. (Perhaps we should call it the
"Excedrin Complex.") But this reaction widens the cultural gap,
making blacks more conscious of their basic differences from whites.
The embarrassment has become even more profound now because
black and white expectation patterns have been broken. Little is
done on either side to relieve the misunderstandings that have led to
the embarrassments. White establishmentarians seem to say that any
dialogues are going to be carried on in their stable, rule-and-settle-
ment–oriented arbitration manner. But black militants, who see
discourse as coercive, are no longer offering that privilege, that accommodation.

The difference is one of the esthetics of performance. The white
order emphasizes victories or settlements as referential things that
may be used as models for the production of new things. The concern is with invention in the face of necessity. But in a very real
sense invention and improvisation, which on the surface seem so
similar to each other, are diametrically opposed—and improvisation
is the model for black activity. Leroi Jones has pointed this out for
us in many different ways. Art in performance, for him (as for all
blacks who share in this process world view) is the model for all
activities—no, that's not even precise, because it is only when viewed
from the esthetician's point of view that the distinction between art
and life needs to be made. In black life, as in black art, it is "the
doing, the coming into being, the at-the-time of" which is crucial.
This is what Jones calls the *verb process* of life and art:

> . . . an artifact made to cohere to preconceived forms, is almost
> devoid of this verb value . . . nothing that already exists is *that* valu-

able. The most valuable quality in life is the will to existence, the un-
connected zoom, which finally becomes in anyone's hand whatever part
of it he could collect. . . . Art-ing is what makes art, but a Being, the
simple noun. It is not a verb but its product. Worship the verb if you
need something. (Jones, 1966, pp. 174–75)

Soul is sass because sass is one of those actions which emphasize
be-ing. It is also any act which confronts, which seizes initiative for
the pleasure of finding energy and letting it throw you around. It is
looseness, but it is also instant reaction. If it doesn't happen to embody our white ideas of the past or the future, and if it doesn't happen to lead us toward what we conceive to be an ideal state of mind,
it has an eternity of its own which resides in the moment of creation.
Soul is willingness and resilience, but it is also pride in knowledge of
the existence of this resilience, and so it is also an *un*willingness to
bend in those directions which don't feel right because to do so is to
deny the existence of such a cultural style and integrity.

So whether a rallying cry or a philosophy of life, the soul movement is at least pointing out that *there is* a black cultural pattern
and that its existence can provide the foundation for the coming-
together operation. Whether blacks will be able to "get their shit
together" remains in question, but if they do, it will certainly be in
the style of soul.

An Afterword

A reader of an earlier form of this book commented that he assumed I had formulated my ideas and then had gone out and found
texts to illustrate my points. I found this strangely flattering though
it was the very opposite of my actual method of operation. My editor
will testify that I suddenly found this book writing me. It poured
out of me from mid-March to mid-May, 1968, and then was revised
in line with some excellent criticism given me by a number of read-
ers, most notably John Szwed. It therefore is constituted of materials conveniently at hand, rather than texts that I collected for the
purpose. But this is "collectanea" which I have lived with as long as
ten years.

My first acquaintance with this kind of black folklore came while I
was living in a ghetto neighborhood in South Philadelphia. I moved
there while a graduate student in folklore at the University of Pennsylvania and lived there nearly two years, in 1958–1960. Being a
folklorist, I simply attempted to record all of the traditional expressive behavior I encountered there. From this came my dissertation "Negro Folklore from South Philadelphia" and later *Deep Down
in the Jungle . . . Negro Narrative Folklore from the Streets of
Philadelphia*, which used only the stories told me by the young men
in the neighborhood. So the texts came first, the explanation and the
theories came later; the theories came because I was troubled at my
inability to understand my neighbors, their culture, and especially

the objectives of their life style and value system. What I attempted to do was not only to place the lore in its cultural setting but to explain on paper the content, style, and structure of the lore and what it reflected of the environment. Being schooled in literature and folklore without any training in social science, I went first to the expressive performances for stylistic analysis, then to surrounding data which imposed itself unwanted on my consciousness. What developed, then, was a method of analysis that remained essentially esthetic in its preoccupations but which I found explaining a great deal more than just esthetic matters. As I found, this was because the role of the performer was so central to an understanding of the status structure and value system of the neighborhood.

My explanations as embodied in that study have not been completely satisfactory to me, especially because things have changed, and I did not take account of the forces for change that I did encounter there. There have been a number of alternative explanations for some of my data which have been asserted in the five years since the book was written, some explanations proposed by the further reading in the social sciences which I've been able to do and others pointed out to me by cogent criticism—most notably by Nat Hentoff and Charles Keil in print and Kenneth S. Goldstein, Bruce Jackson, and again John Szwed, in conversation and correspondence. (I will record my debts to them more particularly in a forthcoming book.) So this is how my method of attack evolved.

It has not changed in the present study. These texts have come to me in the period 1960–68 from a number of sources. Some come from my own brief forays into the field, others from collections handed in by students (mostly blacks), and still others from the students of friends, Dick Reuss and Ed Cray. All of the texts come from lower-class Negro performers except those concerning civil rights. Now, as before, I looked at the content and styles of the texts first to see what was most characteristic in the performance dimension. Then I looked for voiced explanations of the content and style from the talk of the black community itself, an excursion into a kind of folk-esthetics. Then I looked for explanations from a sociological and cultural perspective, using pertinent works by social scientists. Consequently, my hypotheses were arrived at through an analysis of folklore first, society second. But once the ideas were formulated, I felt a necessity to choose illustrations which made my points as effectively as possible. For this, I picked texts which I considered both representative of the repertoire and well-told. This is, after all, a book designed to be read.

This brings up the problem of how representative the texts are, and who they represent. I can only claim that the stories are, by virtue of my experience, characteristic of the repertoires of lower-class young men who tell jokes. But I must note that I have been struck by the number of items in this collection which are well-known and often told both by women and by members of the black bourgeoisie. Young women, it will be noticed, are well represented in the sources of these specific texts. So it is impossible to say just how widespread these patterns are from present data, and therefore I emphasize the male provenience and perspective.

The problem of representativeness also comes up in regard to whether these texts really are the most characteristic stories being told by blacks. Here is where the methods of the folklorist and many sociologists seem to be most divergent. These sociologists seem to want some quantifiable verification of the representative nature of these stories; the only way of establishing this would be by recording a great many more stories than I have, indeed, than I possibly could have. What I, as a folklorist, have looked for, are those motifs, types, stories, motives, which recur often enough to seem characteristic. I look for patterns of repetition and reiteration rather than for sufficiency of data. My only check on this is to take each item which comes from black storytellers and to account for it in the terms outlined here. There *are* numerous stories and story-types which have not been noticed here—but which have been included in *Deep Down in the Jungle* . . . —which do not conform to (or conflict with) the hypotheses given in this study. They are not included because analysis of them would add little to the understanding of the background of the present black situation. This does not mean that I am insensitive to the methodological weaknesses of this approach.

As I stated in the first chapter, I am not trying to argue any causal relationships between black folklore and recent violent and coercive activities. But there are, I am convinced, important and incontrovertible similarities between the two that make the folklore an important tool for an understanding of meaning, style, and motivation. I can only hope that this exercise will explain certain cultural differences that exist between white and black culture and therefore will establish an area of understanding where it did not previously exist. I am not trying to excuse behavior or to explain it away, because I do not think such a job needs to be done. If I eliminate the term and the concept of "cultural deprivation" from the vocabulary of just one person, I'll feel my time on this work has been justified.

Bibliography

Abrahams, Roger D.

    1964. *Deep Down in the Jungle* . . . *Negro Narrative Folklore from the Streets of Philadelphia.* Hatboro, Pa., Folklore Associates.

    1968. "Public Drama and Common Values in Two Caribbean Islands." *Trans-Action,* July/August, 62–71.

Allport, Gordon W.

    1954. *The Nature of Prejudice.* Reading, Mass., Addison-Wesley.

Baldwin, James

    1968. "James Baldwin Tells Us All How to Cool It This Summer." *Esquire* Magazine, July, 49–53, 116.

Beardwood, Roger

    1967. "A Fortune Study of the New Negro Mood." *Fortune* Magazine, January, 145–51, 230–33.

Brown, Claude

    1968. "The Language of Soul." *Esquire* Magazine, April, 88, 160, 162.

Carmichael, Stokely, and Charles V. Hamilton

    1967. *Black Power.* New York, Random House.

Conot, Robert

    1967. *Rivers of Blood, Years of Darkness.* New York, Bantam Books.

Cothran, T. C.

    1951. "Negro Conceptions of White People." *American Journal of Sociology,* Vol. 56, 458–67.

Dahrendorf, Ralf

    1958. "Out of Utopia." *American Journal of Sociology,* Vol. 64, 115–27.

1959. *Class and Class Conflict in Industrial Society.* Stanford, Calif., Stanford University Press.

Darrow, Charlotte and Paul Lowinger

1967. "The Detroit Uprising: A Psychosocial Study." Unpublished ms.

Dollard, John

1937. *Caste and Class in a Southern Town.* New York, Random House (Anchor reprint edition).

Dorson, Richard M.

1967. *American Negro Folktales.* New York, Dell Books.

Duberman, Martin

1968. "Baby, You Better Believe." *New York Times Book Review,* January 21, 8.

Elkins, Stanley M.

1957. *Slavery.* New York, Grosset and Dunlap (1963 reprint edition).

Firestone, Harold

1964. "Cats, Kicks and Color." In *The Other Side* (ed. Howard S. Becker), New York, The Free Press, pp. 281–97.

Fogelson, Robert

1967. "Violence as Protest: An Interpretation of 1960 Riots." Unpublished ms.

Galoob, Debra

1963. "Back in '32 When Times Was Hard." *Riata* (Student literary magazine of the University of Texas) Spring, 24–33.

Goffman, Erving

1967. *Interaction Ritual.* New York, Doubleday and Co.

Gregory, Dick, with Robert Lipsyte

1965. *Nigger.* New York, Pocket Books (reprint edition).

Hannerz, Ulf

1968. "What Negroes Mean by 'Soul'." *Trans-Action,* July–August, 62–9.

Horton, John

1967. "Time and Cool People." *Trans-Action,* April, 5–12.

Hughes, Langston

1966. *The Book of Negro Humor.* New York, Dodd, Mead and Co.

———— and Arna Bontemps

1959. *The Book of Negro Folklore.* New York, Dodd, Mead and Co.

Iceberg Slim

1967. *Pimp, The Story of My Life.* Los Angeles, Calif., Holloway House.

Jansen, William Hugh

1950. "The Esoteric-Exoteric Factor in Folklore." *Fabula: Journal of Folktale Studies,* Vol. 2, 205–11.

Jones, Leroi

1963. *Blues People.* New York, Morrow and Co.

1966. *Home.* New York, Morrow and Co.

Keil, Charles

1966. *Urban Blues.* Chicago, University of Chicago Press.

Leach, E. R.

1954. *Political Systems of Highland Burma.* Boston, Mass., Beacon Press (reprint edition, 1967).

Lester, Julius

1967. "Letter of Resignation to Broadside Magazine." Reprinted in *Sing Out!,* December–January, Vol. 17, No. 6, 41.

Liebow, Elliot

1967. *Talley's Corner.* Boston, Mass., Little, Brown and Co. Portions of this book are reprinted by permission of the publisher. Copyright © 1967 by Little, Brown and Company (Inc.).

Lockwood, David

1956. "Some Remarks on the Social System." *British Journal of Sociology,* Vol. 7, 134–46.

Lomax, Alan

1959. *Blues in the Mississippi Night.* United Artists Record UAL 4027, New York.

Lord, Albert M.

1960. *The Singer of Tales.* Cambridge, Mass., Harvard University Press.

Lowenthal, David

1967. "Race Relations in the British West Indies." *Daedalus,* Spring, 580–626.

Oliver, Paul

1960. *Blues Fell This Morning.* London, Cassell and Co.

Olsen, Jack

1967. *Black Is Best: The Riddle of Cassius Clay.* New York, Dell Publishing Co. (reprint edition). Portions of this book are reprint by permission of G. P. Putnam's Sons and John Cushman Associates, Inc. from *Black Is Best: The Riddle of Cassius Clay* by Jack Olsen. Copyright © 1967 by Jack Olsen.

Owens, Tary

1966. "Poetry from the Texas Prisons." *Riata* (Student literary magazine of the University of Texas), Spring, 22–3.

Paredes, Americo

1967. "Prepared Remarks on Abrahams' and Fogelson's Papers." Unpublished ms.

Rainwater, Lee, and William Yancey

1967. *The Moynihan Report and the Politics of Controversy.* Cambridge, Mass., M. I. T. Press.

Ramsey, Frederic

1950. *Jazz.* "The Blues," Vol. 2. Folkways Record FJ2802, New York.

Riesman, David, Nathan Glazer, and Reuel Denney.

    1950. *The Lonely Crowd.* New York, Doubleday and Co. (reprint, abridged edition).

Simmel, Georg

    1955. *Conflict and the Web of Group Affiliation.* (tr. Kurt H. Wolff and Rinehart Bendix) New York, The Free Press.

Stewart, John

    1823. *A View of the Past and Present State of Jamaica.* Edinburgh, Oliver and Boyd.

Stewart, William A.

    1967. "Sociolinguistic Factors in the History of American Negro dialects," *The Florida FL Reporter,* Vol. 5, No. 2 (Spring).

    1968. "Continuity and Change in American Negro Dialects," *The Florida FL Reporter,* Vol. 6.

Szwed, John

    1966. "Musical Style and Racial Conflict." *Phylon,* Vol. 27, 358–66.

Time Magazine

    1964. "Jazz: the Loneliest Monk." Feb. 28, 84–8.

U.S. Riot Commission

    1968. *Report of the National Advisory Commission on Civil Disorders.* New York, Bantam Books, Inc.

Wallace, Anthony F. C.

    1966. *Religion, and Anthropological Approach.* New York, Random House.

Whinnom, Keith

    1965. "The Origin of European-based Creoles and Pidgins." *Orbis,* Vol. 14, 511–26.

Williams, Robin M., Jr., with John P. Dean and Edward A. Suchman

    1964. *Strangers Next Door: Ethnic Relations in American Communities.* Englewood Cliffs, N.J., Prentice-Hall, Inc.

Wilson, William A.

    1967. "Herder, Folklore, and Romantic Nationalism." Unpublished ms.

Notes on the Texts

1 *An Old Time Story.* Collected from Edward Bryant (age 73),* Austin, Texas, January 1963.

2 *And a New One.* Collected from Greta Lamb, Silsbee, Texas, November 1965.

3 "Two, four, six, eight. . . ." Collected by Luke Etta Hill, Tyler, Texas, from her third grade girls.

4 "This took place. . . ." Collected from Harriet Moore, Austin, Texas, December 1967.

5 "There was this Negro. . . ." Collected from Harriet Moore, Austin, Texas, December 1967.

6 "One time an old. . . ." Collected from Edward Bryant (age 73), Austin, Texas, January 1963.

7 "This colored man. . . ." Collected from James Fortson, Houston, Texas, July 1965.

8 The texts of the boasts and dozens come from my own Philadelphia collection (printed in part in *Deep Down in the Jungle* . . . , pp. 241–242) and from a group of students at Huston-Tillotson College, Austin, Texas, January 1967. These students were from East Texas, Houston, and Chicago.

* Unless otherwise mentioned, all informants were under age 30.

9   *Shine and Stackolee.* Collected from Roosevelt Wattley, Austin, Texas, October 1960.

10   "Back in '32. . . ." Collected from Sidney "Dusty" Walker, Longview, Texas, January 1963.

11   "Now this was down. . . ." Collected from Biddy Brown, Austin, Texas, December 1966.

12   "Did you ever. . . ." Collected from Robert Shaw (age 58), Austin, Texas, September 1965.

13   *Brother Rabbit and Brother Terr'pin.* Collected from Robert Shaw, Austin, Texas, September 1965.

14   "Brother Fox had been. . . ." Reprinted from *Deep Down in the Jungle,* pp. 76–77.

15   "Down South. . . ." Collected from Warnell Jones (from East Texas), Los Angeles, California, 1959.

16   "This here fellow was. . . ." Reprinted from *Deep Down in the Jungle,* pp. 223–224.

17   "Well, once upon. . . ." Collected from Andrea Smith, Marshall, Texas, December 1965.

18   "There once was. . . ." Collected from Arlette Jones, Houston, Texas, December 1965.

19   "There was this nigger. . . ." Collected from John McAffee, Houston, Texas, November 1965.

20   "Three men were sent. . . ." Collected from Ann Tate, Houston, Texas, December 1965.

21   "A man put up a sign. . . ." Collected from Betty Wagner, Prairie View, Texas, December 1965.

22   "Once upon a time. . . ." Collected from Ann Jennings, Dallas, Texas, January 1966.

23   "There was this Nigger. . . ." Collected from Weldon J. Grovey, Sweeny, Texas, July 1965.

24 "One time there was a white man's rooster. . . ." Collected from Curtis Willis (from Florida), Austin, Texas, September 1967.

25 "There was a Mexican. . . ." Collected from Warnell Jones (from East Texas), Los Angeles, California, 1959.

26 *The Great MacDaddy.* Reprinted from *Deep Down in the Jungle,* pp. 162–163.

27 "It was deep down in the jungles. . . ." Collected from Jimmy Bell, Austin, Texas, October 1960.

28 "I'm from the Middle West. . . ." Collected from Sherman Bland, Louisville, Kentucky, January 1967.

29 "Now this was while walking down L.A. street. . . ." Collected from Biddy Brown, Austin, Texas, October 1967.

30 "There was a young boy there. . . ." Collected from Warnell Jones (from East Texas), Los Angeles, California, 1959.

31 "Now this is about a little old country boy. . . ." Reprinted from *Deep Down in the Jungle,* pp. 203–204.

32 "This preacher had a mad crush. . . ." Collected by Weldon J. Grovey, Sweeny, Texas, July 1965.

33 "This preacher he just loved two things in life. . . ." Collected from Vernon Pitts, Sweeny, Texas, July 1965.

34 "This here one's about the time. . . ." Collected from Jerome Lee, Sweeny, Texas, July 1965.

35 "Now this here's about the reverend and the deacon. . . ." Reprinted from *Deep Down in the Jungle,* pp. 251–253.

36 "There was this lady that had two parrots. . . ." Collected from Timothy Grovey, Sweeny, Texas, July 1965.

37 "One Sunday, this preacher. . . ." Collected from Weldon J. Grovey, Jr., Sweeny, Texas, July 1965.

38   "There was this preacher that loved to drink. . . ." Collected from Timothy Grovey, Sweeny, Texas, July 1965.

39   "This preacher would always say. . . ." Collected from Jerome Lee, Sweeny, Texas, July 1965.

40   "I'm gonna Do What They Do To Me," by B. B. King. Recorded on *Blues on Top of Blues* (ABC Records 6011).

41   "Here's to the pussy. . . ." Collected from Sidney "Dusty" Walker, Longview, Texas, January 1963. The other proverbs and toasts here come from my Philadelphia collection, September 1957–August 1960. See my disertation "Negro Folklore from South Philadelphia, A Collection and Analysis" (University of Pennsylvania, 1962).

42   "This old man and his old wife. . . ." Collected from Biddy Brown, Austin, Texas, October 1967.

43   "He Wouldn't Stop Doing It." As recorded in 1930 by Clarence Williams' Novelty Band.

44   "You Dirty Dog," by Clarence Williams. As recorded in 1931 by Clara Smith.

45   From "Roll, Mr. Jelly," by Jelly Roll Morton (I. Cabrez).

46   "Yo-Yo Blues." As recorded in 1929 by Barbeque Bob.

47   "This guy was retired. . . ." Collected from Theopolis J. Lee (age 59), Louisville, Kentucky, December 1967.

47A   "Press My Button," by Lil Johnson.

48   "One time a man had a mule. . . ." Collected from Theodore Roosevelt Brill, Galveston, Texas.

49   "There were three little girls. . . ." Collected from Shirley Williams, Fort Worth, Texas, November 1965.

50   "But don't get me wrong. . . ." Reprinted from *Deep Down in the Jungle,* p. 164.

51 "Over in the Corner sat Sweet Jaw Lucy. . . ." Collected from John R. Grooch, Louisville, Kentucky, January 1967; learned in New Orleans.

52 "Nobody Knows You When You're Down and Out," by Jimmy Cox. Words and music may be found in *The Book of the Blues,* Kay Shirley ed., annotated by Frank Driggs (New York: Crown Publishers, 1963), pp. 87–89.

53 "I used to be rich. . . ." Collected from Burton Ellis, Austin, Texas, September 1966.

54 "You know these two bulls. . . ." Reprinted from *Deep Down in the Jungle,* p. 235.

55 "You know this young dog. . . ." Reprinted from *Deep Down in the Jungle,* pp. 235–236.

56 "Your Friends," by Deadric Malone. Recorded by Bobby "Blue" Bland on *Here's the Man* (Duke Records DLP 75).

57 "Your Friends," by B. B. King. See *Blues on Top of Blues.*

58 "Well, of course, they always. . . ." Collected from Harriet Moore, Austin, Texas, December 1967.

59 "Then there was the story of the southern white man. . . ." Collected from Harriet Moore, Austin, Texas, December 1967.

60 The Hambone routines come from my Philadelphia collection. See my dissertation, "Negro Folklore from South Philadelphia."

61 "Hush Your Mouth." Recorded by Bo Diddley on Chess Records (LP 14131).

62 "Sun Gonna Shine In My Door," by Bill Broonzy. See *The Book of the Blues,* pp. 69–71.

63 "In the Dark," by Lil Green. See *The Book of the Blues,* pp. 8–9.

64 "Well, Dick Gregory. . . ." Collected from Harriet Moore, Austin, Texas, December 1967.

65 "At the start of the riots. . . ." Collected from Charles Colding (social worker), Detroit, Michigan.

66 "Did you hear about the Negro woman. . . ." Collected from Elias Ames, Austin, Texas, September 1966.

67 "This old Negro man. . . ." Collected from Burton Ellis, Austin, Texas, September 1966.

68 "That reminds me of one. . . ." Collected from Elias Ames, Austin, Texas, September 1966.

Index

Acknowledgments

"He Wouldn't Stop Doing It," by Clarence Williams. © Copyright 1930, 1957 by MCA Music, a division of MCA Inc., New York. All rights reserved. Used by permission.

"I'm Going to Do What They Do to Me," by B. B. King. © Copyright 1968. Used with the permission of Pamco Music, Inc., 1330 Ave. of the Americas, New York; Sounds of Lucille, Inc., c/o Sidney Seidenberg, 1414 Ave. of the Americas, New York.

"In the Dark," by Lil Green. © Copyright 1940 by Duchess Music Corporation, New York. All rights reserved. Used by permission.

"Nobody Knows You When You're Down and Out," by Jimmy Cox. © 1922, 1929, 1950, 1956 by MCA Music, a divsion of MCA Inc., New York. All rights reserved. Used by permission.

"Press My Button," by Lil Johnson. © Copyright 1941, 1968 by MCA Music, a division of MCA Inc., New York. All rights reserved. Used by permission.

"Sun Gonna Shine in My Door," by Big Bill Bronzy. © Copyright 1947, 1963 by Duchess Music Corporation, New York. All rights reserved. Used by permission.

"You Dirty Dog," by Clarence Williams. © Copyright 1931, 1958 by MCA Music, a division of MCA Inc., New York. All rights reserved. Used by permission.

"Your Friends," by B. B. King. Used by permission of Modern Music Pub. Inc., New York.

"Your Friends," by Deadric Malone. © Copyright 1962 by Don Music Co. Used by permission.